9-1632

HELEN
KELLER

AMERICAN WOMEN of ACHIEVEMENT

HELEN KELLER

DENNIS WEPMAN

CHELSEA HOUSE PUBLISHERS
NEW YORK • PHILADELPHIA

EDITOR-IN-CHIEF: Nancy Toff
EXECUTIVE EDITOR: Remmel T. Nunn
MANAGING EDITOR: Karyn Gullen Browne
COPY CHIEF: Perry Scott King
ART DIRECTOR: Giannella Garrett
PICTURE EDITOR: Elizabeth Terhune

Staff for HELEN KELLER:

TEXT EDITOR: Marian W. Taylor
ASSISTANT EDITOR: Maria Behan
COPYEDITORS: Gillian Bucky, Sean Dolan
DESIGN: Design Oasis
PICTURE RESEARCH: Sarah Kirshner
PRODUCTION COORDINATOR: Alma Rodriguez
COVER ILLUSTRATION: Lisa Young

CREATIVE DIRECTOR: Harold Steinberg

3 5 7 9 8 6 4

Frontispiece courtesy of the Perkins School for the Blind

Library of Congress Cataloging in Publication Data

Wepman, Dennis. HELEN KELLER.

(American women of achievement)
Bibliography: p.
Includes index.
1. Keller, Helen, 1880–1968—Juvenile literature. 2. Blind-deaf—
United States—Biography—Juvenile literature. [1. Keller, Helen,
1880–1968. 2. Blind-deaf. 3. Deaf. 4. Physically handicapped]
I. Title. II. Series.
HV1624.K4W45   1987   362.4'1'0924 [B] [92]   87-662

ISBN 1-55546-662-1
    0-7910-0417-1 (pbk.)

CONTENTS

AMERICAN WOMEN of ACHIEVEMENT

Abigail Adams
women's rights activist

Jane Addams
social worker

Louisa May Alcott
author

Marian Anderson
singer

Susan B. Anthony
woman suffragist

Ethel Barrymore
actress

Clara Barton
founder of the American Red Cross

Elizabeth Blackwell
physician

Nellie Bly
journalist

Margaret Bourke-White
photographer

Pearl Buck
author

Rachel Carson
biologist and author

Mary Cassatt
painter

Agnes De Mille
choreographer

Emily Dickinson
poet

Isadora Duncan
dancer

Amelia Earhart
aviator

Mary Baker Eddy
founder of the Christian Science church

Betty Friedan
feminist

Althea Gibson
tennis champion

Emma Goldman
revolutionary

Helen Hayes
actress

Lillian Hellman
playwright

Katharine Hepburn
actress

Karen Horney
psychoanalyst

Anne Hutchinson
religious leader

Mahalia Jackson
gospel singer

Helen Keller
humanitarian

Jeane Kirkpatrick
diplomat

Emma Lazarus
poet

Clare Boothe Luce
author and diplomat

Barbara McClintock
biologist

Margaret Mead
anthropologist

Edna St. Vincent Millay
poet

Julia Morgan
architect

Grandma Moses
painter

Louise Nevelson
sculptor

Sandra Day O'Connor
Supreme Court Justice

Georgia O'Keeffe
painter

Eleanor Roosevelt
diplomat and humanitarian

Wilma Rudolph
champion athlete

Florence Sabin
physician

Beverly Sills
singer

Gertrude Stein
author

Gloria Steinem
feminist

Harriet Beecher Stowe
author and abolitionist

Mae West
entertainer

Edith Wharton
author

Phillis Wheatley
poet

Babe Zaharias
champion athlete

CHELSEA HOUSE PUBLISHERS

"Remember the Ladies"

MATINA S. HORNER

Remember the Ladies." That is what Abigail Adams wrote to her husband John, then a delegate to the Continental Congress, as the Founding Fathers met in Philadelphia to form a new nation in March of 1776. "Be more generous and favorable to them than your ancestors. Do not put such unlimited power in the hands of the Husbands. If particular care and attention is not paid to the Ladies," Abigail Adams warned, "we are determined to foment a Rebellion, and will not hold ourselves bound by any Laws in which we have no voice, or Representation."

The words of Abigail Adams, one of the earliest American advocates of women's rights, were prophetic. Because when we have not "remembered the ladies," they have, by their words and deeds, reminded us so forcefully of the omission that we cannot fail to remember them. For the history of American women is as interesting and varied as the history of our nation as a whole. American women have played an integral part in founding, settling, and building our country. Some we remember as remarkable women who— against great odds—achieved distinction in the public arena: Anne Hutchinson, who in the 17th century became a charismatic religious leader; Phillis Wheatley, an 18th-century black slave who became a poet; Susan B. Anthony, whose name is synonymous with the 19th-century women's rights movement, and who led the struggle to enfranchise women; and, in our own century, Amelia Earhart, the first woman to cross the Atlantic Ocean by air.

These extraordinary women certainly merit our admiration, but other women, "common women," many of them all but forgotten, should also be recognized for their contributions to American thought and culture. Women have been community builders; they have founded schools and formed voluntary associations to help those in need; they have assumed the major responsibility for rearing children, passing on from one generation to the next the values that keep a culture alive. These and innumerable other contributions, once ignored, are now being recognized by scholars, students, and the public. It is exciting and gratifying to realize that a part of our history that was hardly acknowledged a few generations ago is now being studied and brought to light.

In recent decades, the field of women's history has grown from obscurity to a politically controversial splinter movement to academic respectability, in many cases mainstreamed into such traditional disciplines as history, economics, and psychology. Scholars of women, both female and male, have organized research centers at such prestigious institutions as Wellesley College, Stanford University, and the University of California. Other notable centers for women's studies are the Center for the American Woman and Politics at the Eagleton Institute of Politics at Rutgers University, the Henry A. Murray Research Center for the Study of Lives, at Radcliffe College, and the Women's Research and Education Institute, the research arm of the Congressional Caucus on Women's Issues. Other scholars and public figures have established archives and libraries, such as the Schlesinger Library on the History of Women in America, at Radcliffe College, and the Sophia Smith Collection, at Smith College, to collect and preserve the written and tangible legacies of women.

From the initial donation of the Women's Rights Collection in 1943, the Schlesinger Library grew to encompass vast collections documenting the manifold accomplishments of American women. Simultaneously, the women's movement in general and the academic discipline of women's studies in particular also began with a narrow definition and gradually expanded their mandate. Early causes such as woman suffrage and social reform, abolition and organized labor were joined by newer concerns such as the history of women in business and the professions and in politics and government; the study of the family; and social issues such as health policy and education.

Women, as historian Arthur M. Schlesinger, jr., once pointed out, "have constituted the most spectacular casualty of traditional history. They have made up at least half the human race, but you could never tell that by looking at the books historians write." The new breed of historians is remedying that omission. They have written books about immigrant women and about working-class women who struggled for survival in cities and about black women who met the challenges of life in rural areas. They are telling the stories of women who, despite the barriers of tradition and economics, became lawyers and doctors and public figures.

The women's studies movement has also led scholars to question traditional interpretations of their respective disciplines. For example, the study of war has traditionally been an exercise in military and political analysis, an examination of strategies planned and executed by men. But scholars of women's history have pointed out that wars have also been periods of tremendous change and even opportunity for women, because the very absence of men on the home front enabled them to expand their educational, economic, and professional activities and to assume leadership in their homes.

The early scholars of women's history showed a unique brand of courage in choosing to investigate new subjects and take new approaches to old ones. Often, like their subjects, they endured criticism and even ostracism by their academic colleagues. But their efforts have unquestionably been worthwhile, because with the publication of each new study and book another piece of the historical patchwork is sewn into place, revealing an increasingly comprehensive picture of the role of women in our rich and varied history.

Such books on groups of women are essential, but books that focus on the lives of individuals are equally indispensable. Biographies can be inspirational, offering their readers the example of people with vision who have looked outside themselves for their goals and have often struggled against great obstacles to achieve them. Marian Anderson, for instance, had to overcome racial bigotry in order to perfect her art and perform as a concert singer. Isadora Duncan defied the rules of classical dance to find true artistic freedom. Jane Addams had to break down society's notions of the proper role for women in order to create new social institutions, notably the settlement house. All of these women had to come to terms both with themselves and with the world in which they lived. Only then could they move ahead as pioneers in their chosen callings.

Biography can inspire not only by adulation but also by realism. It helps us to see not only the qualities in others that we hope to emulate, but also, perhaps, the weaknesses that made them "human." By helping us identify with the subject on a more personal level they help us to feel that we, too, can achieve such goals. We read about Eleanor Roosevelt, for instance, who occupied a unique and seemingly enviable position as the wife of the president. Yet we can sympathize with her inner dilemma: an inherently shy woman, she had to force herself to live a most public life in order to use her position to benefit others. We may not be able to imagine ourselves having the immense poetic talent of Emily Dickinson, but from her story we can understand the challenges faced by a creative woman who was expected to fulfill many family responsibilities. And though few of us will ever reach the level of athletic accomplishment displayed by Wilma Rudolph or Babe Zaharias, we can still appreciate their spirit, their overwhelming will to excel.

A biography is a multifaceted lens. It is first of all a magnification, the intimate examination of one particular life. But at the same time, it is a wide-angle lens, informing us about the world in which the subject lived. We come away from reading about one life knowing more about the social, political, and economic fabric of the time. It is for this reason, perhaps, that the great New England essayist Ralph Waldo Emerson wrote, in 1841, "There is properly no history: only biography." And it is also why biography, and particularly women's biography, will continue to fascinate writers and readers alike.

HELEN KELLER

Blind and deaf since early childhood, Helen Keller, now 23, proudly wears the cap and gown of a college graduate. She earned her degree from Radcliffe College in 1904.

ONE

Night

When 19-year-old Helen Keller of Tuscumbia, Alabama, applied for entrance to Radcliffe College in 1899, she knew she was aiming high. Radcliffe was well known for its high admissions standards; its students were graduates of the best high schools in the United States. Keller had never been to any school at all. She had never studied with other children. For nearly 18 of her 19 years, she had been both blind and deaf.

The entrance tests she took were the same as those given to the other applicants, but hers were written in Braille. A system of printing for the blind, Braille uses combinations of raised dots to represent the letters of the alphabet; the reader interprets them by touch.

Algebra gave her some trouble—it always had—but she won honors in Latin and did as well as the rest of the applicants in other subjects. When the tests were graded she was declared eligible for admission to Radcliffe. All she needed now was the approval of Radcliffe's academic board.

Keller knew some of the college administrators had doubts about admitting a blind and deaf student. In a letter to the board's chairman, she said, "I realize that the obstacles in the way of my receiving a college education are very great—to others they may seem insurmountable; but, dear sir, a true soldier does not acknowledge defeat before the battle."

Radcliffe, the sister school of Harvard, was a conservative institution. Its dean, Agnes Irwin, was not enthusiastic about a change in routine; nor was she optimistic about Keller's chances of success. The handicapped young woman would need unusual services: an interpreter to repeat the lectures to her in finger signs, books in Braille, and a special typewriter for her written work.

Irwin told Keller that Radcliffe was probably not the best place for her, that she might be better off studying on her own than trying to get a regular college degree. The dean was kind but firm. The applicant was polite but equally firm. She thanked Irwin for her advice. Then she renewed her application. Keller was not easily discouraged.

Helen Keller was already well known

Union troops stop Confederate forces at Antietam, Maryland, in 1862. Southern bitterness toward "Yankees" was still strong when Helen Keller was born in Alabama in 1880, 15 years after the Civil War's end.

because of the progress she had made in overcoming her handicaps. While she was waiting to find out if Radcliffe would accept her, she received scholarship offers from Cornell and the University of Chicago, but she declined them both. In a letter to a friend, she admitted that pride had something to do with it. "If I went to any other college," she said, "it would be thought that I did not pass my examinations for Radcliffe."

Blind, deaf, and almost incapable of in-

telligible speech, Keller had faced challenges all her life. She had met them all so far, and she would not give in now. As it turned out, it was Radcliffe that gave in. Its list of incoming freshmen for the fall of 1900 included the name of Helen Keller.

Keller graduated *cum laude* (with honor) from Radcliffe in 1904. Years later, future president Woodrow Wilson asked her why she had been so insistent about going there. "Because," she replied, "they didn't want me at Radcliffe and, being stubborn by nature, I chose to override their objections."

Helen Adams Keller was born on June 27, 1880, the first child of Kate and Captain Arthur Keller. Her father, who had been a Confederate officer in the Civil War, was a wealthy landowner and newspaper publisher in the small town of Tuscumbia, Alabama. Kate and Arthur Keller adored Helen. She was lively, friendly, and, her parents insisted, unusually bright. Her proud father swore she could say "How do you do?" at the age of six months; her mother remembered that by her first birthday, little Helen was "almost" running.

The Keller family's delight in their daughter was not to last. In February 1882, the 19-month-old child was struck by a mysterious illness and a high fever. When her temperature finally dropped to normal, her family wept with relief. Her small, racked body seemed to be recovering its former strength. It was soon clear, however, that something was terribly wrong.

Helen was sleeping badly at night and turning fretfully away from the light in the daytime. The Kellers realized that the high fever had taken an awful toll: Helen was gradually losing her sight and hearing. Modern doctors believe she had had scarlet fever; her own doctors called her sickness "acute congestion of the stomach and brain." Whatever it was, Helen's illness closed her eyes and ears forever.

Arthur Keller, who both owned and edited the local newspaper, was a man of influence in Alabama. In the face of his family's tragedy, however, he was help-

Arthur Keller, Helen's father, held the rank of captain in the Confederate army. After the Civil War, he became editor and publisher of the North Alabamian, *a weekly Democratic newspaper in Tuscumbia.*

less. In a few weeks, Helen was totally blind and deaf; neither her father nor anyone else could help her.

As the days passed, the light faded from Helen's once animated and happy face. She became, as she later described herself, "a phantom," with an "unresponsiveness of tone and look in place of the smile that used to gladden everyone." Existing now in a world of silent darkness, she lost what speech she had learned before her illness. Soon, even the idea of language disappeared. She used a kind of primitive sign language, but the only sounds she made were cries of pain or need and grunts of pleasure.

As Helen grew older and stronger, she became more and more difficult to live with. No one, it seemed, could teach her anything. Her moods alternated between dejection and anger. At the time, many people assumed that anyone blind and deaf was also simpleminded. Some family members recommended that she be committed to a mental institution; her parents, however, refused to consider the idea.

In spite of the barriers between herself and the rest of the world, Helen showed signs of intelligence. When she was very young and still able to see, she had been a clever mimic. Now she began to use signs and signals to express her wishes. She later described them: "A shake of the head meant 'no' and a nod 'yes'; a pull meant 'come' and a push 'go.' Was it bread that I wanted? Then I would imitate the acts of cutting the slices and buttering them. If I wanted my mother to make ice cream for dinner I made the sign for working the freezer and shivered, indicating cold."

Helen represented her father by pretending to put on glasses; pulling her hair into a knot at the back of her head was the sign for her mother. When she wanted to refer to her baby sister Mildred, she stuck her fingers into her mouth; a certain aunt was indicated when Helen tied imaginary bonnet strings under her chin. By the time she was five years old, Helen had a "vocabulary" of about 60 gestures. At least one family member, her

Kate Adams Keller had been a celebrated belle in Memphis, Tennessee, before she married Arthur Keller, 20 years her senior. Helen was their first child.

father's sister Evelina, recognized that Helen was a highly gifted child.

Her intelligence and imagination occasionally added to the difficulties she presented to her family. When she was five years old she learned what keys were for. "One morning," she later recalled, "I locked my mother up in the pantry, where she was obliged to remain three hours, as the servants were in a detached part of the house. She kept pounding on the door while I sat outside on the steps and laughed with glee as I felt the jar of the pounding."

Unfortunately, Helen's mischievous pranks were not the worst of her behavior. The lonely little girl's frustration often expressed itself in explosions of rage. She once found her doll's cradle occupied by her sleeping baby sister. "I grew angry," she later wrote of the incident. "I rushed upon the cradle and overturned it, and the baby might have been killed if my mother had not caught her as she fell."

Keller later wrote, "The desire to express myself grew. The few signs I used became less and less adequate, and my failures to make myself understood were

"Ivy Green," Helen Keller's birthplace, was a simple but comfortable frame house built at the end of a dirt lane in Tuscumbia, Alabama.

17

Samuel G. Howe instructs Laura Bridgman at the Perkins Institution in Boston. Howe's success in teaching the blind and deaf girl to communicate inspired Kate Keller to seek similar help for Helen.

equipped to educate Helen; indeed, most of the family doubted that any school could help her. Kate Keller, however, refused to give up hope. When she read a book called *American Notes*, written in 1842 by British novelist Charles Dickens, she got an idea.

In the book, Dickens described his meeting with Laura Bridgman, a Boston girl who had lost her sight and hearing when she was very young. Laura had lived in an isolated world of darkness and silence until she had met Samuel Gridley Howe. A teacher at the famed Perkins Institution for the Blind in Boston, Howe had managed to teach Laura how to communicate with others by using a "manual alphabet"—letters traced on her palm. Howe had been dead for many years, but, Kate Keller thought, perhaps his methods of teaching could be applied to Helen.

The Kellers had taken their daughter to many specialists, all of whom gave the same unhappy opinion: nothing could restore Helen's sight. Still hoping for a breakthrough, Arthur Keller took six-year-old Helen to visit a Baltimore eye doctor in 1886. Although this expert's diagnosis was no different from that of his predecessors, he said he believed Helen could be educated. Then he made a suggestion that would prove critically important to Helen Keller: why not take the child to Washington, D.C., to see Alexander Graham Bell?

A genius whose many achievements included the invention of the telephone, Bell was deeply interested in the education of the deaf. His development of the telephone had, in fact, grown out of his efforts to teach deaf children to speak.

invariably followed by outbursts of passion. I felt as if invisible hands were holding me, and I made frantic efforts to free myself.

"I struggled—not that struggle helped matters, but the spirit of resistance was strong within me.... After a while, the need of some means of communication became so urgent that these outbursts occurred daily, sometimes hourly."

The Keller family's desperation increased along with their daughter's. There was no school near Tuscumbia

Inventor Alexander Graham Bell (top right) joins teachers and pupils at the Boston School for the Deaf in 1871. It was Bell's advice that led to Annie Sullivan's appointment as Helen Keller's teacher.

Residents of the Perkins Institution for the Blind stroll the balconies of the Boston school in 1904. Annie Sullivan, who had graduated from Perkins in 1886, brought Helen Keller here in 1888.

Keller and his daughter hastened to Washington, where Bell invited them to his home for dinner. Bell, who had an instinctive sensitivity to the problems of the handicapped, warmed to Helen immediately. "He understood my signs," she wrote later, "and I knew it and loved him at once. But I did not dream that that interview would be the door through which I should pass from darkness into light, from isolation to friendship, companionship, knowledge, love."

Bell indeed provided that door. He knew all about American schools for deaf or blind children, and he also knew all about Laura Bridgman, Samuel Howe, and the Perkins Institution. He advised Arthur Keller to write at once to Michael Anagnos, Howe's son-in-law and his successor as director of Perkins. Bell was sure Anagnos could find a suitable teacher for Helen.

Keller wrote the letter, and Anagnos soon replied. He said he found Helen's case very interesting because of its similarities to Laura Bridgman's and that he would begin to look for the right teacher immediately. The Kellers waited with impatient excitement for Anagnos's next letter.

The letter finally arrived, and it contained good news. Anagnos had, he reported, found a teacher who was "exceedingly intelligent, strictly honest, industrious, [and] ladylike in her manner." Furthermore, said the Perkins director, the candidate was "familiar with Laura Bridgman's case and with the methods of teaching deaf, mute, and blind children." He assured the Kellers that the woman he was recommending would "make an excellent instructress and most reliable guide for your little daughter."

The woman Anagnos had picked was 21-year-old Annie Sullivan, the daughter of poor Irish immigrants. Abandoned by her parents at the age of nine, she had been sent to the state poorhouse in Tewksbury, Massachusetts. Here she had spent five years among people rejected by society—alcoholics, orphans, the elderly, and the insane. Almost blind as a result of an eye disease she had suffered when she was very young, Sullivan had been unable to read or write until she was a teenager.

At the age of 14, Annie Sullivan had been accepted at Perkins. There she had undergone an eye operation that restored much of her sight, and had learned to read. Sullivan had just graduated at the head of her class. She was well acquainted with the problems of the blind and had spent many hours with the aging Laura Bridgman, who was still living at Perkins.

Born in 1866, Annie Sullivan was illiterate and almost blind when she entered the Perkins Institution in 1880. After six years of eye operations and intensive education, she became the best student in her class.

Although Sullivan had fine qualifications and was enthusiastically recommended by Anagnos, Arthur and Kate Keller were somewhat apprehensive about her background. They were, however, desperately eager to find a teacher for Helen, and they told the Perkins director they would accept Sullivan. They would, they said, pay her $25 per month, and "would treat her as one of our immediate family."

Howe's education of Laura Bridgman had been an important chapter in the history of education. When Annie Sullivan nervously stepped out of the carriage in Tuscumbia, Alabama, on March 3, 1887, a new chapter in that history—and in the story of the human spirit—began.

Using the manual alphabet, Annie Sullivan and Helen Keller converse in 1890. The two were a perfect match: Sullivan was a brilliant teacher, and Helen was a very fast learner.

TWO

Sunrise

Anne Mansfield Sullivan had no more experience in teaching than Helen Keller had in learning, but she was determined to give herself to the job with her whole heart. She had never surrendered to despair, although her life so far had been a hard and lonely one.

Sullivan's worst problem had been her eyes. When she was two years old she had contracted trachoma, a virus that causes hard lumps inside the eyelid. These lumps scratch and scar the eyeball, often causing blindness. By the time Sullivan had gone to the poorhouse at Tewksbury, she could barely see; two operations performed while she was there did nothing to help her.

One dream had kept young Annie from losing hope: someday, she swore to herself, she would go to school. Everyone had always told her this was impossible; schools were not for poor children like her, and with her eyes, she could never learn to read and write, anyway. Nevertheless, she held fast to her dream.

When a committee from the Massachusetts State Board of Charities visited Tewksbury to investigate conditions at the poorhouse, Annie broke away from the other inmates and ran up to the visitors. "I want to go to school!" she shouted. The chairman of the committee was R. F. Sanborn, a Boston philanthropist (a person who helps those in need with money or work). He asked the frantic girl a few questions, but her burst of courage had ebbed and she was unable to speak further.

Sanborn had been impressed by Annie's desperate plea. When he left the poorhouse, he inquired into her case and then recommended that she be sent to the Perkins Institution. When she heard the news, Annie could hardly believe her good luck. Perkins was the best-known school for the blind in the United States. It was also very expensive. Most of its students were the children of wealthy New Englanders with good educational backgrounds. Annie, whose parents had been poor and illiterate, could not even write her name.

The courage and determination that had enabled Annie to plead for a chance to go to school helped her to survive there. A charity case among rich and privileged students, she became an independent loner, often defying both her fellow students and her teachers. More than once, director Michael Anagnos was urged to expel the "impudent" girl from the school.

Annie's first friend—and for some time her only companion—was the deaf and blind Laura Bridgman, now more than 50 years old. Although Bridgman could communicate by spelling and "reading" words with her fingers, she had never become self-sufficient enough to leave Perkins for a life on her own. She and

The grim exterior of the state poorhouse in Tewksbury, Massachusetts, suggests the kind of existence shared by its inmates. Annie Sullivan spent five years of her childhood here.

Annie spent many evenings in conversation, making finger signs on each other's palms.

Bridgman knew little about the outside world, but she taught Annie things the girl could have learned from no one else. Annie came to understand the secret, silent universe where Bridgman had lived for so long, and she learned the methods by which Howe had brought light into that universe 40 years earlier.

The eye operation that Annie received when she was 16 restored much of her sight. She no longer really belonged at an

At the age of 15, Annie Sullivan was independent, headstrong, and defiant. During her first year at Perkins, director Michael Anagnos called her "Miss Spitfire."

institution for the blind, but because she had no family, no money, and no way to make a living, she was allowed to remain. In her seven years at Perkins she had changed from an awkward, illiterate child into a poised, articulate young woman. When she graduated, in 1886, she was first in her class and was chosen as valedictorian—the student who delivers the class speech at the graduation ceremony.

Michael Anagnos was convinced that Sullivan was the ideal person to serve as teacher and companion to the blind-deaf girl in Alabama. When he told her about the job, she was both excited and frightened. It was an unusual opportunity, and she knew her own experience with blindness and her close association with Laura Bridgman had prepared her well for such a position.

On the other hand, Sullivan was uneasy about leaving Boston and the people she knew. Alabama was a long way off, and she had no idea what the Kellers would be like. Furthermore, the Civil War had ended only 22 years before, and she knew that the defeated South still regarded Northerners with suspicion.

After considering both sides of the question, Sullivan decided to accept the challenge. For six months she strained her still weak eyes, reading and rereading the files that Howe had written about the Bridgman case. At last, in the spring of 1887, Sullivan felt she was ready.

Sophia Hopkins, a longtime Perkins staff member who had become Sullivan's close friend and confidante, assembled a modest wardrobe for the teacher-to-be. Anagnos lent Sullivan money for the long train trip from Boston to Alabama. The blind children at Perkins, as excited as Sullivan, pooled their allowances to buy a doll for Helen; Laura Bridgman, an expert with needle and thread, supplied its clothes. The doll went into Sullivan's trunk along with a board for writing Braille and several books with raised letters.

Her eyes still sore from yet another operation, this one performed a short time before her departure from Perkins, Annie Sullivan said goodbye to all she had known. Then she boarded the train for Tuscumbia.

Seven-year-old Helen Keller cradles a pet dog at her home in Tuscumbia. Such quiet moments were rare for the little girl, who often displayed uncontrollable rage at her own helplessness.

Sightless from the age of three, Frenchman Louis Braille invented a raised alphabet for the blind in 1826. His system — known as Braille — is still in use.

Helen, a half-savage child with wild hair and an expression of sullen defiance, was not a very encouraging prospect for a teacher. Nevertheless, Sullivan could hardly wait to meet her. Interrupting Arthur Keller's formal speech of welcome, she bent to wrap the blind child in her arms. Helen thought her mother was hugging her; when she realized it was someone else, she squirmed away. "I remember how disappointed I was when the untamed little creature stubbornly refused to kiss me and struggled to free herself from my embrace," Sullivan later recalled.

She also recalled her surprise at Helen's appearance. "I had expected to see a pale, delicate child," she said in a letter to Sophia Hopkins. "But there's nothing pale or delicate about Helen. She is large, strong, and ruddy, and as unrestrained in her movements as a young colt."

Helen's moods changed quickly; moments after she had escaped from her new teacher's embrace she approached her again and was soon running her fingers over the young woman's face. Then Helen snatched Sullivan's handbag and began to search it for candy. When her mother took the purse away, Helen flew into a tantrum, rolling on the ground and screaming. Sullivan offered her pocket watch as a distraction, and Helen finally stopped crying. The child's signs of curiosity were encouraging.

No one present at the meeting three days later ever forgot it. Almost seven decades later, on Keller's 75th birthday, she said, "My birthday can never mean as much to me as the arrival of Anne Sullivan on March 3, 1887. That was my soul's birthday." She recalled having a feeling that day that "something unusual was about to happen." She spent most of the afternoon on the front porch, "dumb, expectant."

Even more heartening was the speed with which Helen understood Sullivan's message that there would be candy later. Sullivan told Hopkins about it in a letter: "There was a trunk in the hall," she wrote, "and I led Helen to it and, by using her signs, tried to tell her that I had a trunk like it, and in it there was something very good to eat. She understood, for she put both her hands to her mouth and went through the motions of eating something she liked extremely, then pointed to the trunk and me, nodding emphatically."

The next morning, full of hope, Sullivan began her first lesson. She patterned it after Howe's early work with Bridgman. First she spelled a word onto Helen's hand with the finger alphabet used by deaf-mutes. Then she demonstrated the meaning of the word with an object or an action. Her first word was "doll," which she illustrated by presenting Helen with the gift from the blind children at Perkins. Helen liked the new "game," and she immediately began to mimic Sullivan's actions.

The game was a success—but it was not accomplishing its objective. "I did not know that I was spelling a word, or even that words existed," Keller recalled later. "I was simply making my fingers go in monkey-like imitation."

For weeks Helen "made her fingers go," still unaware of any connection between

The Kellers' water pump still stands in Tuscumbia; here, in 1887, Helen Keller first grasped the concept of language. At that moment, Keller wrote later, "my heart began to sing."

their movements and words. When she was bored or tired, her temper flared. At one such point she hurled her new doll to the floor, smashing it to pieces. She showed no regret. "I had not loved the doll," she wrote later. "In the still, dark world in which I lived there was no strong sentiment or tenderness."

"The greatest problem I shall have to solve," said Sullivan in a letter to Hopkins, "is how to discipline and control [Helen] without breaking her spirit. I shall go rather slowly at first and try to win her love." Sullivan's firm yet gentle approach would be effective in the long run, but its immediate results were less than pleasant. A week after she had told Hopkins about her plans, she lost two front teeth, knocked out by Helen in one of her fits of rage.

Arthur and Kate Keller, at a loss to know how to deal with their tragically handicapped daughter, had never even tried to discipline her. Helen had always had her own way in everything. If she resisted bathing and grooming, she re-

Helen practices the manual alphabet on Jumbo, one of the Keller family's setters. Once she had discovered language, the little girl "talked" constantly.

mained dirty and uncombed. If she wanted breakfast at midnight, the family had bacon and eggs by the light of the moon. At family meals Helen was permitted to help herself to whatever she wanted from anyone's plate.

Sullivan considered this child-raising policy—or lack of one—a serious mistake, but she had no wish to argue with the Kellers. However, she knew that without some discipline Helen would never make any progress. One morning things came to a head.

When Helen reached for a piece of food on her teacher's plate that day, Sullivan slapped the child's hand. Astonished, Helen tried again. She got another slap. The Kellers were upset by the teacher's stern behavior, but grudgingly willing to let her test her theories, they left the dining room. In a letter to Hopkins, Sullivan described the scene that followed:

"I locked the dining room door, and proceeded to eat my breakfast, though the food almost choked me. Helen was lying on the floor, kicking and screaming and trying to pull my chair from under me. She kept this up for half an hour, then she got up to see what I was doing. I let her see that I was eating, but did not let her put her hand in the plate.

"She pinched me, and I slapped her every time she did it. Then she went all around the table to see who was there, and finding no one but me, she seemed bewildered. After a few minutes she came back to her place and began to eat her breakfast with her fingers. I gave her a spoon, which she threw on the floor. I forced her out of her chair and made her pick it up.

"Finally I succeeded in getting her back in her chair again, and held the spoon in her hand, compelling her to take up the food with it. . . . It was another hour before I succeeded in getting her napkin folded. . . . I suppose I shall have many such battles with the little woman before she learns the only two essential things I can teach her, obedience and love."

Since Helen's family had always let her do exactly as she pleased, teaching "obedience" was not going to be easy. "To get her to do the simplest thing," Sullivan told Hopkins, "such as combing her hair or washing her hands or buttoning her boots, it was necessary to use force, and, of course, a distressing scene followed. The family naturally felt inclined to interfere, especially her father, who cannot bear to see her cry."

At last the strain became unendurable, and Sullivan put her foot down. Either she and Helen would move out of the main house and away from the family for a while, she told the Kellers, or she would leave. Helen's father objected to Sullivan's insistence on disciplining his daughter, and he was not pleased with her new plan. "I have a great mind," he told his wife, "to send that Yankee girl back to Boston."

At last, however, even Arthur Keller saw that if Sullivan was not given a free hand in educating Helen, the whole project would fail. He gave his consent, and Helen and her teacher went to live in a small cottage on the Keller farm. There, the teacher-pupil relationship improved quickly.

On March 20, a week after the move, Sullivan wrote Hopkins: "My heart is sing-

Despite her handicaps, Helen Keller was an outgoing and attractive girl. In an 1891 report, Michael Anagnos noted that she had "beautiful brown hair falling in luxuriant curls over her pretty shoulders."

ing for joy this morning. A miracle has happened! . . . The wild little creature of two weeks ago has been transformed into a gentle child. She is sitting by me as I write, her face serene and happy, crocheting a long red chain of Scotch wool. She learned to stitch this week, and is very proud of the achievement."

"She lets me kiss her now," the letter continued, "and when she is in a particularly gentle mood, she will sit in my lap for a minute or two. . . . The great step—

the step that counts—has been taken. The little savage has learned her first lesson in obedience. . . . It now remains my pleasant task to direct and mould the beautiful intelligence that is beginning to stir in the child-soul."

Helen continued to spell words out on her teacher's palm; it was a game she enjoyed, but she still did not connect the words with the objects they stood for. "She has no idea yet," noted Sullivan, "that everything has a name."

One day Helen's father brought Belle, the family dog, to the cottage. Helen threw her arms around Belle's neck and began to play with one of the setter's paws. "We couldn't think for a second what she was doing," Sullivan reported later, "but when we saw her make the letters 'd-o-l-l' on her own fingers, we knew that she was trying to teach Belle to spell."

Two weeks after she "learned her first lesson in obedience," Helen received the first great insight of her life. On April 5, 1887—a date neither she nor Sullivan would ever forget, and one that would become famous in the history of education—Helen Keller broke through the darkness that surrounded her. She discovered human language.

Helen and her teacher had had a hard morning struggling with a lesson, and Helen was impatient and angry. At last Sullivan gave up and decided to take her pupil for a walk. They headed for the water pump at the wellhouse. Helen Keller described the incident in her book, *The Story of My Life*:

"Someone was drawing water, and my teacher placed my hand under the spout.

As the cool stream gushed over one hand, she spelled into the other the word *water*, first slowly, then rapidly. I stood still, my whole attention fixed upon the motions of her fingers. Suddenly I felt a misty consciousness as of something forgotten—a thrill of returning thought; and somehow the mystery of language was revealed to me.

"I knew then that 'w-a-t-e-r' meant the wonderful, cool something that was flowing over my hand. That living word awakened my soul, gave it light, hope, joy, set it free! There were barriers still, it is true, but barriers that could in time be swept away.

"I left the wellhouse eager to learn. Everything had a name and each name gave birth to a new thought. As I returned to the house, every object which I touched seemed to quiver with life."

The teacher was as thrilled as her pupil. In a letter she wrote Hopkins that day, Sullivan said that after Helen had spelled the word "water" several times, "she dropped on the ground and asked for its name and pointed to the pump and trellis, and suddenly turning around she asked for my name." Sullivan had then slowly spelled "t-e-a-c-h-e-r" into Helen's palm; from that moment on, she was "Teacher" to Helen and to the world.

Once Helen started to learn, there was no stopping her. When the baby-nurse brought Helen's sister Mildred into the wellhouse, Helen triumphantly spelled "baby" and pointed to the nurse. Before the end of the day, Sullivan told Hopkins, Helen had learned 30 new words, including "door," "open," "shut," "give," "go," and "come."

Mildred Keller (right) leans affectionately on her sister Helen. The girls were close friends. In one of her earliest letters, Helen wrote, "Mildred is a dear little sister, and we have happy times together."

The next morning, Sullivan reported to Hopkins, Helen got up "like a radiant fairy. She has flitted from object to object, asking the name of everything and kissing me for very gladness." Helen had spent five years in lonely darkness. Now, little more than a month after Sullivan's arrival in Tuscumbia, she began to sense the dawn of a new day.

Helen, always fond of flowers, holds a bouquet of lilies of the valley in this 1890 portrait. Deprived of sight and hearing, she had unusually acute senses of taste, smell, and touch.

THREE

Morning

After Sullivan and her pupil had lived in their own cottage for a few weeks, they returned to the main house and the rest of the family. Helen's progress continued to be rapid. Three months after she had "discovered" language, she knew more than 300 new words. Equally important, she could use them accurately. She began to construct simple but understandable sentences, which she eagerly spelled on her teacher's receptive hand.

Sullivan used none of the day's accepted teaching methods. She preferred to let the child acquire language as normal children do, by observation and imitation. To Sullivan, traditional systems of education seemed "to be built up on the supposition that every child is a kind of idiot who must be taught to think. Whereas," she declared, "if the child is left to himself, he will think more and better."

Everyday objects around the farm fascinated the newly awakened little girl. She learned to tell one kind of flower from another by running her fingers over their petals and stems, and she came to know the names of many. During one of their walks, she and "Teacher" came upon a bubbling spring. When Sullivan told her that squirrels came there to drink, Helen named the spring "squirrel-cup."

The two occasionally came across dead animals in the woods, and Sullivan allowed Helen to touch them so she would know what they were like. She noted that the little girl was very anxious to "see" what she called a "walk-squirrel"—a live one. One day the teacher brought her pupil to a nest where a chicken was hatching eggs. She explained the process to Helen and let her hold a shell in her hand so she could "feel the chicken 'chip, chip.'" To her friend Hopkins, Sullivan wrote that Helen's "astonishment, when she felt the tiny creature inside, cannot be put in a letter." Sullivan was both amused and touched when Helen, introduced to a baby pig, asked to feel the shell from which the piglet had emerged.

Everything was new and wonderful to the little girl, and her teacher shared her enchantment. "I feel," said Sullivan to Hopkins, "as if I had never seen anything till now."

One morning a highly excited Helen

came racing into her teacher's room. Over and over, she spelled "dog—baby" and then counted off five of her fingers. At first Sullivan thought a dog had hurt Helen's little sister Mildred, but Helen's happy face satisfied her that nothing was wrong. At last she allowed Helen to bring her to the wellhouse; there she found one of the family dogs with five newborn puppies.

Sullivan spelled out the word "puppy" to Helen. When the little girl pointed to each of the tiny animals and then to each finger on one hand, Sullivan taught her the word "five." One of the puppies was much smaller than the others, and Helen spelled out "small." Sullivan expanded by spelling *very* small."

All the way back to the house, Sullivan reported to Hopkins, Helen kept using the new word: "One stone was 'small,' another was 'very small.' When she touched her little sister, she said 'Baby—small. Puppy—*very* small.'"

Helen was so enthusiastic about her new vocabulary that she often "talked" to herself, spelling words and phrases on her own hand. By May 1887, Sullivan decided her pupil was ready to learn to read. She had brought with her from Perkins a few simple books whose words were printed with raised letters, enabling them to be "read" with the fingertips.

To teach Helen how to use these books, Sullivan first spelled each letter in the child's palm, then pressed her fingertips to a piece of cardboard on which the letter had been embossed. In one day, Helen learned the whole raised alphabet and could read any word she already knew. Using a special frame to hold words, she learned to arrange them in simple sentences; from here it was only a short step to Sullivan's books.

Once more, teacher and pupil made a game of learning. They often perched in a tree near the house while they worked. Sitting side by side on a branch, they competed to see which could first spot words that Helen knew. The little girl's delight in the lessons was boundless. "When her fingers light upon words she knows," wrote Sullivan, "she fairly screams with pleasure and hugs and kisses me for joy, especially if she thinks she has me beaten."

Helen soon learned all she could from the few books Sullivan had brought with her; they needed more books, but material printed in raised type was expensive and hard to get. In response to Sullivan's request, Michael Anagnos of the Perkins Institution supplied a special series of words printed on stiff paper for Helen's use.

The words included the names of Keller family members and of farm implements and animals familiar to Helen. When the package of embossed words arrived in Tuscumbia, Helen at once set them in her own frame and began to make sentences. She could, it seemed, never get enough of the game.

By June Helen had learned to write. She could not, of course, see what she produced, but she was able to make readable letters with a pencil, keeping them even by using a writing board marked with deep horizontal lines. Using her left hand to guide her right, she stayed within the grooves and reproduced the letters she had felt on the stiff pages of her books. In a few weeks, she had mastered the

Perched in a favorite spot, teacher and pupil discuss a new book in 1904. Using a tree as a classroom had been one of Sullivan's earliest inspirations.

"square-hand" script that was taught to the blind children at Perkins.

Helen's first letter, proudly written on June 17, was addressed to her cousin Anna. It contained no capital letters or punctuation marks, but it was clear. It said: "helen write anna george will give helen apple simpson will shoot bird jack will give helen stick of candy doctor will give mildred medicine mother will make mildred new dress"

Helen's amazing progress impressed everyone who knew her, even those relatives who had urged the Kellers to "put her away" as a mental defective. One of these family members, Kate Keller's brother Fred, admitted the child had improved radically—but he never gave "that Yankee girl" any credit for Helen's transformation.

Even more impressed was Michael Anagnos. He proudly included Sullivan's letters about Helen in the annual reports of the Perkins Institution, and wrote her warm letters full of advice and support.

Helen's success—which, Anagnos well

This "square-hand" script is part of a letter Keller wrote when she was 12 years old. Although she could write clearly, Keller preferred to compose in Braille, so she could read back what she had written.

knew, was Sullivan's success—was very important to him. Sullivan was, after all, a graduate of Perkins, and whatever credit she received as a teacher of the blind must reflect on his school and himself. He thought of Helen Keller as a second Laura Bridgman, the blind-deaf girl who had made Perkins famous a half-century earlier.

Sullivan understood how Anagnos felt, but his extravagant praise made her uneasy. "I am glad Mr. Anagnos thinks so highly of me as a teacher," she wrote Hopkins, "but 'genius' and 'originality' are words we should not use lightly."

However nervous she was about public recognition for her work, Sullivan knew what she had accomplished so far. To Hopkins she wrote, "I want to say something for your ears alone. Something within me tells me I shall succeed beyond my dreams. Were it not for some circumstances that make such an idea highly improbable, even absurd, I should think Helen's education would surpass in interest and wonder Dr. Howe's achievement."

Sullivan's letter to Hopkins went on to discuss her pupil's "remarkable powers," and to express her fear that too much attention could harm her. She was, insisted Sullivan, "no ordinary child," and the public's interest in her education would therefore "be no ordinary interest." Because of this, said the teacher to her friend, "let us be exceedingly careful what we say and write about her. . . . You must promise never to show my letters to anyone. My beautiful Helen shall not be transformed into a prodigy [child genius] if I can help it."

On exhibit at Perkins Institution, this Boston Braille Writer — a "typewriter" for the blind — was made in 1910. The first machine for writing Braille was introduced in 1892.

To those close to Helen and her teacher, the harmony between the two was obvious. Tuscumbia, however, was an old-fashioned, typically southern small town; some of its more conservative residents disapproved of Sullivan's outspoken "Yankee" manner and independent attitude.

The summer of 1887 was scorching; most Alabamians drooped in the heat, and Helen was no exception. Many of Sullivan's critics blamed Helen's pale face and thin frame on Sullivan, asserting that the teacher was "overtaxing" the child's brain. Sullivan, already impatient with Tuscumbia's narrow ways, found this attitude infuriating.

"I am sure the heat, and not the beautiful, natural activity of [Helen's] mind is responsible for her condition," she fumed to Hopkins. "We are bothered a good deal by people who . . . tell us that Helen is 'overdoing,' that her mind is too active (these very people thought she had no mind at all a few months ago!) and suggest many absurd and impossible reme-

Annie Sullivan's heroic role in Helen Keller's life was deeply appreciated by Helen's parents. Many other family members, however, refused to see anything good about this stubborn "Yankee girl."

Dr. Samuel Gridley Howe, a pioneering educator of the blind, was also a staunch abolitionist. He was married to Julia Ward Howe, author of "The Battle Hymn of the Republic."

dies. But so far nobody seems to have thought of chloroforming her, which is, I think, the only effective way of stopping the natural exercise of her faculties."

As soon as the weather cooled off, Helen's appetite returned. Her tantrums had disappeared entirely and her thirst for information increased. "There is seldom a cloud seen on her face and we observe that it grows brighter each day," reported Sullivan just before Helen's seventh birthday.

At the end of July, Helen began to learn Braille, her hardest challenge so far. This system of writing for the blind, devised in 1826 by Louis Braille, a French teacher of the blind, consists of arrangements of raised dots representing letters and combinations of letters. It is written with a pointed instrument called a stylus, which is used to punch the dots into stiff paper.

Because many dots are required for each word, Braille is a slow method of writing, but Helen took to it at once. She much preferred it to the angular, square-hand printing she did with a pencil because she could read what she wrote. Sullivan, who had never mastered the Braille system, read and wrote it awkwardly, and Helen soon surpassed her teacher.

Helen's capacity for fun increased along with her ability to communicate. In November she went to her first circus, enjoying it as much as any child with sight and hearing. The circus performers found Helen as interesting as she found them. They let her feed the elephants and take a ride on the biggest one. She stroked the lion cubs, marveling at their gentleness. When she was told they would grow fierce as they got older, she said, "I will take the baby lions home and teach them to be mild."

It seemed that if anyone could have done that, Helen could. A leopard licked her hand, and a huge black bear held out his paw, which she shook with grave courtesy. She was delighted with the monkeys; when one of them tried to steal the flowers from her hat, she laughed along with the audience. "I don't know who had the best time," said Sullivan later, "the monkeys, Helen, or the spectators." When she kissed all the circus performers to show her appreciation, some of them cried.

There were no tears that Christmas, however. For the first time, Helen took part in the festivities, and it was the happiest holiday the Kellers had ever had. Helen hung up her stocking—in fact, just to make sure Santa Claus saw it, she hung up two—and was thrilled to find them filled on Christmas morning. She was especially pleased when she unwrapped a Braille slate and paper. "I will write many letters," she said happily, "and I will thank Santa Claus very much."

Sullivan did not always see eye to eye with the Kellers, but this Christmas both parents were profoundly moved by the sight of their daughter's radiant face. Arthur Keller took Sullivan's hand in silence—"more eloquent than words," she recorded—and Kate Keller's eyes were filled with tears. "I never realized until this morning," she said to Sullivan, "what a blessing you have been to us." That morning, at least, Sullivan and the Kellers were one happy, loving family.

(text continues on page 46)

An 1890 photograph of Perkins students includes Helen Keller (standing at left) and Tommy Stringer (lower right). Helen had raised the money to educate Tommy, a deaf and blind five-year-old, at Perkins.

IN HELEN KELLER'S OWN WORDS

The world I see with my fingers is alive, ruddy, and satisfying. Touch brings the blind many sweet certainties which our more fortunate fellows miss, because their sense of touch is uncultivated. When they look at things, they put their hands in their pockets.

It is interesting to observe the difference in the hands of people. They show all kinds of vitality, energy, stillness and cordiality.... Mark Twain's hand is full of whimsies and the drollest humors, and while you hold it the drollery changes to sympathy and championship.

Through the sense of touch I know the faces of friends, the illimitable variety of straight and curved lines, all surfaces, the exuberance of the soil, the delicate shapes of flowers, the noble forms of trees, and the range of mighty winds.

I have just touched my dog. He was rolling on the grass, with pleasure in every muscle and limb. I wanted to catch a picture of him in my fingers, and I touched him as lightly as I would cobwebs. . . . He pressed close to me, as if he were fain to crowd himself into my hand. . . . If he could speak, I believe he would say with me that paradise is attained by touch; for in touch is all love and intelligence.

The senses assist and reinforce each other to such an extent that I am not sure whether touch or smell tells me the most about the world. Everywhere the river of touch is joined by the brooks of odor-perception. Each season has its distinctive odors. The spring is earthy and full of sap. July is rich with the odor of ripening grain and hay. As the season advances, a crisp, dry, mature odor predominates, and goldenrod, tansy, and everlastings mark the onward march of the year. In autumn, soft, alluring scents fill the air, floating from thicket, grass, flower, and tree, and they tell me of time and change, of death and life's renewal, desire and its fulfillment.

After my education began the world which came within my reach was all alive. I spelled to my blocks and my dogs. I sympathized with plants when the flowers were picked, because I thought it hurt them, and that they grieved for their lost blossoms. It was years before I could be made to believe that my dogs did not understand what I said, and I always apologized to them when I ran into or stepped on them.

Without imagination what a poor thing my world would be! My garden would be a silent patch of earth strewn with sticks of a variety of shapes and smells. But when the eye of my mind is opened to its beauty, the bare ground brightens beneath my feet, and the hedge-row bursts into leaf, and the rose-tree shakes its fragrance everywhere.

The calamity of the blind is immense, irreparable. But it does not take away our share of the things that count — service, friendship, humor, imagination, wisdom. It is the secret inner will that controls one's fate. We are capable of willing to be good, of loving and being loved, of thinking to the end that we may be wiser. We possess these spirit-born forces equally with all God's children.

Necessity gives to the eye a precious power of seeing, and in the same way it gives a precious power of feeling to the whole body. Sometimes it seems as if the very substance of my flesh were so many eyes looking out at will upon a new world created every day. The silence and darkness, which are said to shut me in, open my door most hospitably to countless sensations that distract, inform, admonish, and amuse. With my three trusty guides, touch, smell, and taste, I make many excursions into the borderland of experience which is in sight of the city of Light.

I am sure that if a fairy bade me choose between the sense of sight and that of touch, I would not part with the warm, endearing contact of human hands or the wealth of form, the mobility and fullness that press into my palms.

Our blindness changes not a whit the course of inner realities. Of us [the blind] it is as true as it is of the seeing that the most beautiful world is always entered through the imagination. If you wish to be something you are not — something fine, noble, good — you shut your eyes, and for one dreamy moment you are that which you long to be.

In January 1888 Sullivan received a copy of the Perkins annual report. It made her sound almost like a saint, and she was not pleased. "I appreciate the kind things Mr. Anagnos has said about Helen and me," she wrote Hopkins, "but his extravagant way of saying them rubs me the wrong way. . . . How ridiculous to say I had drunk so copiously of the noble spirit of Dr. Howe that I was fired with the desire to rescue from darkness and obscurity the little Alabamian! I came here simply because circumstances made it necessary for me to earn my living."

Even worse in Sullivan's eyes were the stories about her and Helen that had begun to appear in Boston newspapers. Their exaggerated reports left her torn between anger and amusement. "One paper," she said, "has Helen demonstrating problems in geometry by means of her playing blocks. I expect to hear next that she has written a treatise on the origin and future of the planets!"

In May Anagnos invited Helen and her teacher to visit the Perkins school. Sullivan was delighted; the trip would mean a temporary escape from the little southern town where she felt like an outsider. It would also give her a chance to see her friends in Boston. Most important, it would expose Helen to a larger world, allow her to meet other blind children, and give her the opportunity to use the school's extensive resources.

Helen was as excited as her teacher about visiting Boston. Months earlier, she

Taking part in a gym class in the early 1900s, a Perkins teacher and her students practice throwing a basketball. Then as now, the school tried to help its students develop all their capabilities.

had written a letter to the "dear little blind girls" at Perkins, promising that she would come to see them. "Helen and blind girls will have fun," the seven-year-old had said in her letter, happily noting that "blind girls can talk on fingers."

With her mother and her teacher, Helen boarded the train for Boston in late May. On their way north, Sullivan tapped out a steady stream of words on Helen's hand, describing the countryside, the flocks of sheep, the cotton fields, the farmers in their fields, to the fascinated little girl. In Washington, the travelers stopped to see Alexander Graham Bell, the inventor whose recommendation of the Perkins Institution had led to Sullivan's arrival in Tuscumbia.

Bell, who had devoted much of his life to helping the handicapped, had kept up with Helen's progress, but he was surprised to discover how well the little girl had learned to communicate. "Her achievement," he proclaimed, "is without parallel in the education of the deaf." Bell's enthusiastic comments were reported by the press, adding to Helen's growing celebrity.

Helen, in fact, had become so famous that the president of the United States asked to meet her. "We went to see Mr. [Grover] Cleveland," Helen wrote. "He lives in a very large and beautiful white house. . . . Mr. Cleveland was very glad to see me."

When she arrived at Perkins, Helen was elated. It was one thing for the president of the United States to be very glad to see her—she was used to adults making a fuss over her—but quite another to meet a crowd of children like herself.

Laura Bridgman, the blind-deaf subject of Samuel G. Howe's educational breakthrough, reads Braille at Perkins. Cool and remote at 58, Bridgman scolded eight-year-old Helen Keller for being "forward."

"It delighted me inexpressibly," she recalled years later, "to find that they knew the manual alphabet. What a joy to talk to other children in my own language! Until then I had been like a foreigner speaking through an interpreter. In the school where Laura Bridgman was taught, I was in my own country."

The blind children greeted their twice-handicapped visitor warmly. They invited her to join their games and, their fingers tapping the words into her palm, told her all about life at Perkins. The school's library contained the largest collection of books for the blind in the United States, and Helen pounced on them, eagerly running her hand across their pages.

At Perkins Helen finally met Laura Bridgman, now 58 years old. Although she did not fully understand it at the time, Helen owed a great deal to Bridgman. This blind and deaf woman, she wrote later, had "bridged the chasm between mankind and me." She went on to wonder what her own life might have been like if Samuel Howe "had not had the imagination to realize that the immortal spirit of Laura Bridgman had not died when her physical senses were sealed up."

Bridgman gave Helen a kiss, but when the impetuous child touched her face—as she always did when she met someone new—the blind woman drew back. "You must not be forward when calling on a lady," she spelled out primly. Helen later described her reaction to Bridgman: "To me, she seemed like a statue I had once felt in a garden. She was so motionless and her hands were so cool, like flowers that had grown in shady places."

After Perkins closed for the summer, Helen, Kate Keller, and Annie Sullivan went to visit Sophia Hopkins at Cape Cod. Hopkins and Helen soon became fast friends. Hopkins introduced the little girl to the ocean, which enchanted her. "I could never stay long enough on the shore," Helen wrote later. The "sea air was like a cool, quieting thought" and "the buoyant motion of the water filled me with an exquisite, quivering joy." When she emerged from her first dip, she had one question: "Who put salt in the water?"

Helen returned to Tuscumbia in the fall, her skin tanned, her body healthy, her appetite for learning keener than ever. "Teacher" could hardly keep up with her endless requests for information. Sullivan's eyes, never strong, began to trouble her again, however. It soon became clear that she needed another operation, which meant another trip to Boston. She decided to bring Helen along so she could spend the winter of 1888–89 at Perkins.

Helen never enrolled as a regular student at Perkins, but she and her teacher spent the next four winters there as Anagnos's guests. Helen was taught how to model in clay, and she began to learn French. She loved the idea of speaking foreign languages and managed to persuade the busy director to tutor her in his native Greek.

Helen benefited from the lessons of the teachers at Perkins, but her education was still—literally—in Sullivan's hands. Helen's fluency with her fingers was amazing; her speed was clocked at 80 words per minute, and Sullivan was the only teacher who could keep up with her.

Immensely proud of the part his institution had played in Helen's education, Anagnos spread the word about her wherever he went. Despite Sullivan's disapproval, he always spoke and wrote of the child as though she were almost supernatural. He called her "the eighth wonder of the world," an "intellectual prodigy," and "a marvel."

Visiting his native Greece, Anagnos paid a call on Queen Olga, to whom he read one of Helen's letters. According to the Perkins director, the Greek monarch listened to Helen's description of a rose garden and cried. Queen Victoria of England was also familiar with Helen's story, learning of it through a magazine article sent to her by Alexander Graham Bell. By the time Helen was 12 years old, her name was familiar to people all over the world.

Largely through Anagnos's efforts, Helen met the leading intellectuals of Boston, among them poet Oliver Wendell Holmes, who wrote of his surprise at Helen's mastery of English. She charmed them all. American newspapers began to call her "the wonder girl" and "the miracle."

In 1890 one of Laura Bridgman's former teachers returned from Europe with some exciting news. She had met a Norwegian girl, like Helen blind and deaf from infancy, who had learned to speak. There was nothing physically wrong with Helen's voice, and she was immediately fired with a new determination. Into Sullivan's hand she spelled, "I must speak."

Afraid that studying speech would lead to bitter disappointment for Helen, Sullivan opposed the idea at first, but Helen was insistent. At last the teacher agreed to take her pupil to see Sarah Fuller, principal of Boston's Horace Mann School for the Deaf. Fuller was impressed with Helen's spirit, and she agreed to take on the job of teaching her to talk.

"She passed my hand lightly over her face," Helen recalled, "and let me feel the position of her tongue and lips when she made a sound. I was eager to imitate every motion and in an hour had learned six elements of speech: M, P, A, S, T, and I."

Learning to speak was a slow, painful process. After 10 lessons Helen was able to grunt a sentence to Sullivan: "I am not

Perkins director Michael Anagnos gives Helen a hug in mid-1891. Anagnos had praised Helen to the skies, but before the year was over, he had accused her of plagiarism and broken off his friendship.

dumb now." It was an achievement, but only Fuller and Sullivan could understand the words.

Except for a word or two in her infancy, Helen had never spoken. Her vocal cords were healthy, but they were weak and untrained for speech. Today a voice specialist would give child like Helen exercises to develop volume and control before encouraging her to speak, but in 1890 such techniques were unknown.

Helen never learned to speak clearly. Fuller taught her to lip-read by touching

49

the lips and throats of people speaking to her, but she never achieved natural pitch, volume, or enunciation.

Many who listened to her said they could only hear her consonants, and inventor Thomas Edison later said that her voice reminded him of "steam exploding." The only people who seemed to have no trouble understanding Helen Keller's speech were—perhaps unsurprisingly—children.

Helen's inability to learn to speak clearly would be a source of regret for the rest of her life. Except for this disappointment, however, her time at Perkins continued to be happy and productive. She was admired by many people, as much for her generous nature as for her intelligence.

In 1890 a friend wrote to her about Tommy Stringer, a deaf and blind five-year-old who had been sent to live in a poorhouse in Pennsylvania. Eager to bring him to Boston and get him a teacher, Helen wrote to friends and newspapers, asking for money to help the boy. Her efforts raised $1,600; young Tommy soon arrived in Boston, where he was accepted at the Perkins Institution.

Helen's achievements were receiving even more attention than Laura Bridgman's had half a century earlier. In the 1891 annual report of the Perkins school, Anagnos devoted more than 200 pages to Helen Keller. Her sunny relationship with the enthusiastic director was not, however, to last much longer.

In November 1891 Helen sent her friend Anagnos a fairy tale full of poetic images. Called "The Frost King," it was, said Helen, "a little story which I wrote for your birthday gift." Anagnos was delighted. He called the effort Helen's "second miracle" and had it published. Soon, however, Anagnos's delight turned to dismay. It was discovered that "The Frost King" was strikingly similar to a story published in 1873.

Anagnos set up a "trial" and required Helen to stand alone while eight school representatives cross-examined her for two hours. The miserable child agreed that her story was much like the earlier one, but she said she had no memory of the first version. She concluded that the story must have been read to her once and that "long after I had forgotten it, it came back to me so naturally that I never suspected that it was the child of another mind."

It finally turned out that a copy of the first version had been in the Cape Cod house where Helen had stayed three years earlier. Four of the eight "judges" believed that Helen had no idea the story was not her own; the other four said she was guilty of plagiarism—stealing the work of another.

Anagnos cast a tie-breaking vote of "not guilty," but he later reversed his position, breaking off his relationship with both Helen and her teacher. He never mentioned their names in his reports again.

"As I lay in my bed that night [after the "trial"]," Helen later wrote, "I wept as I hope few children have wept. I felt so cold, I imagined I should die before morning. . . . I think if this sorrow had come to me when I was older, it would have broken my spirit beyond repairing."

Author Mark Twain had long been one of Helen's admirers. When he read about

Author Mark Twain was infuriated by charges that Helen Keller had plagiarized a story. "I couldn't sleep," he wrote, "for blaspheming about it."

Rejected by her friend Michael Anagnos after the 1891 plagiarism "scandal," Helen Keller shares a quiet moment with the ever-loyal Annie Sullivan.

the investigation into her story, he was both outraged and bitterly amused. "Oh, dear me, how unspeakably funny and owlishly idiotic and grotesque was that 'plagiarism' farce!" he wrote. "To think of those solemn donkeys breaking a little girl's heart with their ignorant damned rubbish!"

Twain called the judges "a collection of decayed human turnips . . . a gang of dull and hoary pirates piously setting themselves the task of disciplining and purifying a kitten that they think they've caught filching a chop." But the episode was anything but funny to Helen.

The charge of plagiarism cast a shadow that would darken her life for years. In the autobiography she wrote in 1902, she said, "I have never played with words again for the mere pleasure of the game. Indeed, I have ever since been tortured by the fear that what I write is not my own."

In spite of her unhappiness about the "Frost King" episode, Helen managed to be philosophical. "This sad experience," she wrote, "may have done me good and set me thinking on some of the problems of composition. My only regret is that it resulted in the loss of one of my dearest friends, Mr. Anagnos." Eleven-year-old Helen had defended herself as well as she could. Now she returned to Tuscumbia, disappointed but not defeated.

Keller enjoys the scent of a rose as she reads Braille. Her sense of smell was keen. One friend even claimed that Keller could determine the color of a rose "with one whiff."

FOUR

Day

Helen Keller resumed her life in Alabama with optimism. "Everything had budded and blossomed," she wrote of her homecoming. "I was happy." Nevertheless, when the editor of *The Youth's Companion*, a popular weekly magazine, wrote to ask her for an autobiographical sketch, she hesitated. "The thought that what I wrote might not be absolutely my own tormented me," she recalled. Eager to help restore her pupil's self-confidence, Sullivan urged her to take the assignment.

Helen finally agreed. She wrote a brief account of her life entitled "My Story," and sent it to the magazine. The *Companion*'s editor, much impressed with the piece, sent its author a check for $100— an unusually high fee for the time. He published it with an introductory note: "Written wholly without help of any sort by a deaf and blind girl, 12 years old, and printed without change." Readers responded to "My Story" with enthusiasm. And no one questioned its originality.

Helen's family and friends were concerned about her further education. Arthur Keller had never been a very good

businessman. His financial position had been steadily declining, and by 1893 he was barely able to support his wife and children, let alone pay Sullivan's meager salary. Keller not only stopped paying her, he began to borrow money from her.

Alexander Graham Bell had been devoted to Helen from the day he met her, and he deeply admired her teacher. As Arthur Keller's fortunes declined, the inventor increased his attentions to Helen. She should, he thought, be exposed to all the experiences of a normal child.

Bell took Helen to the zoo in Washington and escorted her and Sullivan to Grover Cleveland's second presidential inauguration in 1893. The following spring, he sent Sullivan and Helen to Niagara Falls. Helen was awed by "the wonders and beauties" of the tremendous cataracts. "It is difficult to describe my emotions," she wrote, "when I stood on the point which overhangs the American Falls and felt the air vibrate and the earth tremble."

When Helen was 13, she spent three weeks with Bell and Sullivan at the World's Columbian Exposition, a mam-

Visiting Niagara Falls in 1893, Keller (center) conveys her excitement to Sullivan (left). The couple at right are friends of Alexander Graham Bell; he sponsored the trip but was unable to go himself.

ues, uncut diamonds, a Viking ship, telephones and phonographs. Everything enchanted her—except, she recalled, "the Egyptian mummies, which I shrank from touching." During her visit, she wrote,"I took in the glories of the fair with my fingers." And, she added, "I took a long leap from the little child's interest in fairy tales and toys to the appreciation of the real and the earnest in the workaday world."

In the summer of 1894 Bell made a speaking engagement for Annie Sullivan. She was to address a prestigious organization called the American Association to Promote the Teaching of Speech to the Deaf. By now Sullivan was well known among educators of the handicapped, and the organization was eager to hear her explain the methods she had used in teaching Helen.

Helen accompanied her teacher to the meeting, held in Chautauqua, New York. The American Association was very important to Bell, and it turned out to be important to Sullivan and her pupil as well. At the meeting, they met John D. Wright and Thomas Humason, educators who were preparing to open a special school for the deaf in New York City.

moth world's fair held in Chicago in the summer of 1893. The exposition, honoring Columbus's discovery of America four centuries earlier, was a celebration of America's technological progress. Helen was stunned by exhibits from India, Egypt, Europe, the New World.

Given permission to touch whatever she chose, Helen eagerly examined stat-

Wright and Humason, who had developed new methods of instruction, believed they could teach Helen to speak naturally, and perhaps even to sing. Helen's hopes rose. She wanted desperately to be able to talk as other people did.

Bell, too, was hopeful. He asked John Spaulding, a Boston philanthropist who had long been interested in Helen, to underwrite her tuition at the new school. Spaulding quickly complied. In October

BOSTON
HOME JOURNAL

A PAPER OF TO-DAY

OLD SERIES, VOL. 40.
NEW SERIES, VOL. 10.   No. 49.   BOSTON, SATURDAY, DECEMBER 5, 1896.   PER ANNUM, $2.50.
SINGLE COPIES, 5 CENTS.

Keller appears on the cover of the Boston Home Journal *in 1896. Public interest in the courageous deaf-blind girl resulted in innumerable newspaper and magazine articles, many of them wildly exaggerated.*

1894 Helen eagerly signed the registration book at the Wright-Humason Oral School; there she and Sullivan stayed for the next two years.

Along with speech and lip-reading, Helen studied arithmetic, geography, French, and German. The speech lessons were not successful, however. Helen's voice remained toneless and unmodulated, still almost impossible for most people to understand. "I suppose we aimed too high," she wrote sadly, "and disappointment was therefore inevitable." Despite this setback, she did well in her academic subjects, particularly German and geography.

Helen and her deaf classmates went on field trips all over New York City. They visited the Statue of Liberty, Central Park, and the rocky cliffs across the Hudson River. They attended a variety of events ranging from dog shows to Broadway musicals. They were also taken to the city's slum neighborhoods, where Helen got her first real-life insights about the poor and underprivileged.

Helen's new acquaintances included members of New York's society, theatrical, and literary circles. Most of them had heard stories about this gifted blind girl, and they were eager to meet her and her teacher.

Helen charmed everyone she met, from millionaire industrialists Andrew Carnegie and John D. Rockefeller to popular stage stars Ellen Terry and Joseph Jefferson. She was befriended by Edward Everett Hale, a prominent clergyman, and by writers like Mark Twain and William Dean Howells. Twain, of course, had championed Helen during the "Frost

A pensive Keller sits by a stream near her home in Tuscumbia. As a child, she had been frightened when left alone, but as she grew older she began to appreciate moments of solitude.

King" controversy, but they had not met face-to-face until now.

Helen and her teacher adored Twain, who returned their affection. Said Helen of Twain, "I feel the twinkle in his eye in his handshake." Said he, "The two most interesting characters in the 19th century are Napoleon and Helen Keller."

Helen, who had loved Twain's *Life on the Mississippi* and *Huckleberry Finn*, spent hours listening to the celebrated author talk. He never condescended to her, but occasionally he would gently move her hand from his lips, saying, "Now Helen, I must curse."

Twain was always quick to defend his young admirer. He once heard a man pitying Helen because of the "dullness" of her life. "You're damned wrong there!" the author snapped. "Blindness is an exciting business, I tell you; if you don't believe it, get up some dark night on the wrong side of bed when the house is on fire and try to find the door."

In 1896 Helen's kind benefactor John Spaulding died without leaving a will; the income on which Helen and Sullivan had been living was now cut off. Arthur Keller, in debt and no longer able to contribute to his daughter's support, suggested that she leave school and become a stage performer.

Everyone close to Helen was horrified by her father's idea. Sullivan's old friend Sophia Hopkins said his proposal to take Helen away from her studies and "show her as you would a monkey" was "dreadful." Kate Keller said she would die before she would permit such a thing. Fortunately, Helen had made some powerful friends; they now came to her aid.

Alexander Graham Bell and Mark Twain organized a campaign to finance Helen's education. Just as she had once asked people for money to help young Tommy Stringer, her admirers approached wealthy acquaintances on her

Helen Keller accomplished many of the goals she set for herself, but one of her most cherished dreams was forever unrealized: despite enormous effort, she never learned to speak clearly.

behalf. In a letter to an oil-company executive, Twain wrote, "It won't do for America to allow this marvelous child to retire from her studies because of poverty. If she can go on with them, she will make a name that will endure in history for centuries."

The campaign was a success; enough money was raised to pay for the completion of Helen's education. This news was, however, offset by sadness. In the summer of 1896, Helen and her teacher were visiting Hopkins in Massachusetts when they learned of Arthur Keller's sudden death in Alabama.

"My father is dead," Helen wrote to Alexander Graham Bell. "He died last Saturday at my home in Tuscumbia and I

Mark Twain's stern look masks his deep affection for Keller. Twain also admired Sullivan. "It took the pair of you," he told Keller, "to make a complete and perfect whole."

was not there. My own dear loving father! Oh, dear friend, how shall I bear it!" She had never known, Helen wrote, "how dearly I loved my father until I realized that I had lost him."

Sullivan wrote to a friend, "Poor Helen is heartbroken. We had no idea that anything was wrong till Friday and the end came in a few hours. Helen was frantic with grief and her one desire was to get to her mother." Sullivan's letter went on to explain that Kate Keller had asked Helen not to come home, "as it was the beginning of their sickliest season." This, observed Sullivan, "was another blow to Helen and she is still inconsolable."

Her father's death left Helen even more determined to learn to stand on her own two feet. After two years at the Wright-Humason school, she was ready to think about college. She made up her mind—in spite of what she later called the "strong opposition of many true and wise friends"—to enroll in a "regular" school, one whose other students could see and hear. She and Sullivan selected the Cambridge School for Young Ladies, a Boston institution where she could prepare for the Radcliffe entrance examinations.

Arthur Gilman, the director of the Cambridge School, opposed the idea of admitting the 16-year-old blind and deaf Keller. His school, he told Sullivan, had no facilities for "special" students, and he doubted that Keller could keep up with the other young women. Grudgingly, he finally agreed to meet the prospective student—and changed his mind on the spot. Amazed by, as he put it, "this marvelous girl," he accepted her; Keller entered the Cambridge School in September 1896.

For the next year Keller followed the regular course of study at the Cambridge School—Greek and Roman history, literature, French, German, Latin, and mathematics—with Sullivan always at her side to spell the lessons in the finger alphabet. The two lived in a school dormitory where, except for Sullivan's presence, Keller lived the same life as the other students.

She thoroughly enjoyed life with her "normal" classmates. "I joined them in many of their games," she wrote later, "even blindman's buff and frolics in the snow; I took long walks with them; we discussed our studies and read aloud the things that interested us. Some of the girls learned to speak to me, so that Miss Sullivan did not have to repeat their conversation."

Keller did well in her studies and passed all her year-end examinations. She began her second year at Cambridge full of hope, ready for another full schedule of classes. Gilman, however, had other ideas. Convinced that she was working much too hard, he decided she should take fewer courses and spend an extra year at the school before applying to Radcliffe.

Sullivan disagreed with Gilman. She believed Keller could handle the work with ease. Perhaps, she suggested, the director wanted to prolong Keller's stay at his school because of the favorable publicity she brought to it. Gilman responded by accusing Sullivan of driving her pupil toward a state of collapse.

What began as a difference of opinion turned into a battle. Sullivan infuriated Gilman by criticizing him in front of other

(text continues on page 62)

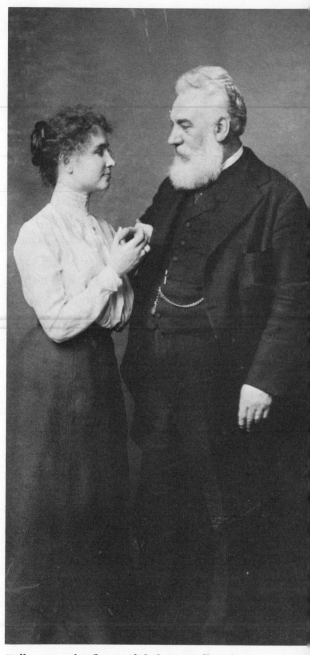

Keller uses the finger alphabet to talk to her good friend Alexander Graham Bell. Bell's lifelong interest in the deaf had led to his invention of the telephone in 1876.

Using a Braille writer, college freshman Keller prepares an assignment at Radcliffe in 1900. In addition to mastering this special machine, Keller became skilled on a standard typewriter.

Facing page: Braille, a system of touch reading and writing for the blind, uses raised dots arranged in "cells." A 63-character alphabet is formed by arranging the dots in different positions or combinations.

UNDERSTANDING BRAILLE

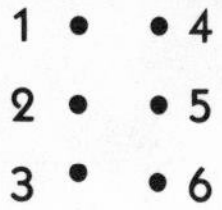

```
1 •   • 4
2 •   • 5
3 •   • 6
```

LINE 1
a b c d e f g h i j 
1 2 3 4 5 6 7 8 9 0

Line 1, consisting of the first 10 letters of the alphabet, is formed with dots 1,2,4,5 in the upper part of the braille cell. When preceded by the numeric indicator these cells have number values.

LINE 2 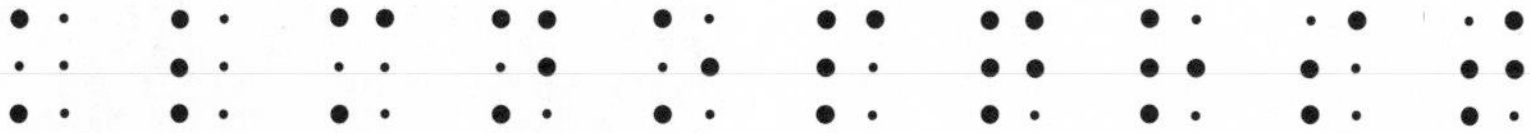
k l m n o p q r s t

Line 2 adds dot 3 to each of the characters of Line 1.

LINE 3 
u v x y z and for of the with

Line 3 adds dots 3 and 6 to each of the characters of the first line.

LINE 4 
ch gh sh th wh ed er ou ow w

Line 4 adds dot 6 to each of the characters of the first line.

LINE 5 
, ; : . en ! ( ) "/? in "

Line 5 repeats the characters of Line 1 in the lower portion of the cell, using dots 2,3,5,6. Most of the characters have punctuation values.

LINE 6 
st ing # ar ' -

Line 6 is formed with dots 3,4,5,6.

LINE 7 
general accent sign | used for two-celled contractions | italic sign; decimal point | letter sign | capital sign

Line 7 is formed with dots 4,5,6.

Although punctuation and letter values are given for each configuration, most of the configurations have other meanings when used in conjunction with different Braille characters.

teachers and students. Gilman in turn provoked Sullivan's wrath by accusing her of endangering Keller's health by overworking her. Finally, Gilman wrote Kate Keller; her daughter's well-being, he said, depended on an immediate separation from her teacher. Confused and distressed by Gilman's reports, Kate Keller sent him a telegram authorizing him to act as her daughter's guardian.

The news devastated Helen. After the telegram had arrived, she wrote later, she realized that "something terrible had happened. 'What is it, Teacher?' I cried in dismay. 'Helen, I fear we are going to be separated.' 'What! Separated? What do you mean?' I said, utterly bewildered." After Sullivan explained the situation, she walked away from the school in despair. Keller reported that as her teacher had passed the Charles River in Boston, "an almost overmastering impulse seized her to throw herself in the water."

Regaining her self-control, Sullivan fired off a telegram of her own. Addressed to Kate Keller, its message was short and clear: "We need you." That was enough to bring the frantic mother to Boston on the next train. She confronted Gilman and removed her daughter from his school.

"I found Mr. Gilman had made cruel use of the authority I had given him," Kate Keller wrote later. "I certainly never dreamed of Miss Sullivan being forced away from Helen. . . . Helen is in perfect physical condition and if she shows any evidence of nervous prostration or over-work I cannot discover it." Helen Keller and Annie Sullivan were reunited. No one ever tried to separate them again.

Phiz, a bull terrier given to Keller by her Radcliffe classmates, gets a hug from his mistress. Keller loved dogs and would own many, but she always remembered Phiz with special affection.

Keller and her teacher stayed with friends in Wrentham, near Boston, for the next two years. A tutor worked with them to finish the work the Cambridge School had begun, and in 1899 Keller was ready to take the entrance tests for Radcliffe. The tests contained queries that might baffle many scholars, let alone a 19-year-old woman who had been blind and deaf for most of her life.

Among the questions were: "Where are the following: Arbela, Coryere, Dacia, Lade, Rubicon, Trasimene, and with what famous events is each connected?" Part of the English test said: "Write a paragraph or two on *Silas Marner*. On the coming of Eppie. On the death of Gabriel. Tell the story of *The Merchant of Venice*, showing how many and what stories are interwoven in it."

Keller passed with flying colors; her certificate of admission even noted that she "passed with credit in Advanced Latin." Unable to convince her that college might be too difficult, Radcliffe admitted her in the fall of 1900. She was by now a poised and confident young woman. She had proved that she could do what others could do—and more.

At Radcliffe, Keller received no special consideration for her handicaps. She got excellent grades and so impressed her English professor that he showed her compositions to friends and colleagues. In 1902, the editor of the *Ladies' Home Journal* asked her to write the story of her life for the magazine.

At first Keller said no. Signed up for the same number of classes as the other students, she was already working very hard. Keller also had the added labor of rushing home after every lecture and transcribing in Braille what she could remember of Sullivan's finger-alphabet translations.

The editor of the *Journal* was persistent. He pointed out that Keller had already written much of her life story—a story no one else in the world could tell—in her college themes. She would need only to reorganize the themes for the magazine piece. Furthermore, he said, the *Journal* would pay $3,000—more than the average American made in a year—for the story. For a young woman aching to be self-sufficient, this was a very persuasive argument.

Encouraged by Sullivan, Keller signed a contract with the magazine and began to write "The Story of My Life." John Macy, a young Harvard instructor and an editor of the magazine *The Youth's Companion*, agreed to edit the work. He was deeply impressed with the young blind woman's ability to put together her manuscript.

"Her memory of what she had written was astonishing," Macy wrote later. "She remembered whole passages, some of which she had not seen for many weeks, and could tell, before Miss Sullivan had spelled into her hand a half-dozen words of the paragraphs under discussion, where they belonged and what sentences were necessary to make the connections clear."

The trio—Keller, Sullivan, and Macy—worked well together, and the first installment of "The Story of My Life" was mailed to the *Ladies' Home Journal* on schedule. The magazine's editors, delighted with what Keller had written, published it in April 1902. It was followed by four more installments.

In 1903 the manuscript was expanded into a book. It consisted of three parts: Keller's autobiography, a selection of her letters, and an account of her education, written by Macy and including many of Sullivan's letters and comments. *The Story of My Life* got glowing reviews; it was, said one critic, "full of force, individuality, and charm." The *San Francisco Chronicle* said, "It seems to be the style of a practiced writer rather than that of a college girl," and *The Literary Digest* praised it for its lack of "morbidness or self-pity."

The reviewers also recognized Annie Sullivan's role. The *New York Sun* reminded its readers that "the wonderful

(text continues on page 66)

FROM

A CHANT OF DARKNESS

BY HELEN KELLER

Once in regions void of light I wandered;
In blank darkness I stumbled,
And fear led me by the hand;
My feet pressed earthward,
Afraid of pitfalls.
By many shapeless terrors of the night affrighted,
To the wakeful day
I held out beseeching arms.

Then came Love, bearing in her hand
The torch that is the light unto my feet,
And softly spoke Love: "Hast thou
Entered into the treasures of darkness?
Hast though entered into the treasures of the night?
Search out thy blindness. It holdeth
Riches past computing."

The words of Love set my spirit aflame.
My eager fingers searched out the mysteries,
The splendors, the inmost sacredness, of things,
And in the vacancies discerned
With spiritual sense the fullness of life;
And the gates of Day stood wide.

I am shaken with gladness;
My limbs tremble with joy;
My heart and the earth
Tremble with happiness;
The ecstasy of life
Is abroad in the world.

My hands evoke sight and sound out of feeling,
Intershifting the senses endlessly;
Linking motion with sight, odor with sound
They give color to the honeyed breeze,
The measure and passion of a symphony
To the beat and quiver of unseen wings.
In the secrets of earth and sun and air
My fingers are wise;
They snatch light out of darkness,
They thrill to harmonies breathed in silence.

I walk in the stillness of the night,
And my soul uttereth her gladness.
O Night, still, odorous Night, I love thee!
O wide, spacious Night, I love thee!
O steadfast, glorious Night!
I touch thee with my hands;
I lean against thy strength;
I am comforted.

O fathomless, soothing Night!
Thou art a balm to my restless spirit,
I nestle gratefully in thy bosom,
Dark, gracious mother!
Like a dove, I rest in thy bosom.
Out of the uncharted, unthinkable dark we came,
And in a little time shall return again
Into the vast, unanswering dark.

~~feat of dragging Helen Keller out of her~~ hopeless darkness was only accomplished by sacrificing for it another woman's whole life." Mark Twain said he was "enchanted" by the book. "You are a wonderful creature," he said in a letter to Keller, "the most wonderful in the world—you and your other half together—Miss Sullivan, I mean, for it took the pair of you to make a complete and perfect whole."

The influential magazine *The Century* called *The Story of My Life* "unique in the world's literature." The public agreed. The book is still read in 50 languages.

Just before Keller graduated from Radcliffe in 1904, she and Sullivan bought an old farmhouse in Wrentham, purchasing it with money earned by *The Story of My Life*. The "wonder-child" was now 24 years old. It was time to decide what she would do with her life. What form her career would take she did not yet know, but she was sure of one thing: "I shall devote my life to those who suffer from loss of sight."

Her typewriter was never silent. With the assurance of a successful author, Keller wrote one magazine article after another, discussing the prevention of blindness, the education of the blind, and the special problems they faced. Sullivan worked at her side, reading her pages back to her so she could expand and revise them. John Macy often visited the women, offering his editorial assistance.

Sullivan's eyes, never strong, were growing worse. "Without John's assistance, I fear we could not have managed," wrote Keller to a friend. Macy's help, she said, meant that "Teacher does not have

Keller moves her sensitive hands over a piece of sculpture, the art form she appreciated most. Sullivan encouraged her pupil to try sculpture herself, but Keller did not enjoy it. She preferred reading.

to use her eyes half as much as she did last year." The young man had become an important part of the household. Soon Keller sensed that he and "Teacher" were falling in love.

Macy asked Sullivan to marry him. She refused. She was, she argued, 11 years older than he; in any case, she could never abandon her beloved Helen. He kept on asking and she kept on saying no. She told Keller she would never marry. "Oh, Teacher," Keller recalled saying, "if you love John and let him go, I shall feel like a hideous accident!"

Macy assured Sullivan he would never come between her and Keller. The teacher, who had denied herself a personal life for so many years, could resist no longer; she married Macy in 1905. After a brief honeymoon, the couple settled down in Wrentham with Keller.

The next several years were calm and productive for Keller and the Macys. All three were busy writing; Macy, who continued to work for *The Youth's Companion*, was also finishing a book about author Edgar Allan Poe. The trio lived fairly comfortably, but despite their hard work, money was always in short supply. Writing brought fame but little cash.

Keller's writing was largely about herself; her own life was not only the subject she knew best, it was what magazine editors and readers wanted to hear about. In 1908 she published *The World I Live In*, a series of essays explaining how she compensated for her lack of vision and hearing by using her other senses.

The book was an instant success. Professor Charles T. Copeland of Harvard,

As Sullivan (right) reads over John Macy's shoulder, Keller talks to him through the finger alphabet. Although Sullivan refused Macy's proposals at first, he was persistent; they were married in 1905.

Keller's former teacher, wrote her about it. "Fate narrowed the world you live in," he said, "but you have burst the bonds of fate and contrived to make us . . . think better of the world." Critics referred to Keller as a "genius," and the eminent psychologist and philosopher William James called the essays "psychological classics."

Keller was naturally pleased with the warm reception of *The World I Live In*, but she was growing tired of writing about her own problems. "I found myself," she wrote later, "utterly confined to one subject—myself, and it was not long before I had exhausted it."

In 1909 John Macy joined the Socialist party, which was then undergoing a pe-riod of surging popularity. Led by the charismatic Eugene V. Debs, the party was attracting thousands of new members, their occupations ranging from farmer to college professor, their incomes from pennies to millions.

Keller had long been distressed about poverty and its effects on American children. She had also become a staunch suffragist—an advocate of women's right to vote. The principles of the Socialist party, as explained by Macy, paralleled her own, and she too joined the party. (Sullivan was the minority member of the household. Politically conservative, she distrusted both socialism and suffragism.)

Keller now began to write about controversial subjects like women's rights; she even discussed such "unmentionable" subjects as infant blindness caused by venereal disease. She marched in a "Votes For Women" parade, and lectured and wrote about economic reforms and the conditions of the working class.

In 1909 the country was in the grip of inflation, and the residents of the Wrentham household were finding it increasingly difficult to manage. Nevertheless, when millionaire philanthropist Andrew Carnegie offered to give Keller a lifetime annual pension of $5,000, she politely refused it. Accepting money for herself when she saw so many others in true need was not in keeping with her newly acquired social philosophy. "I already have a fair share," Keller wrote, "and millions have less than their rightful portion."

In 1913 Keller published *Out of the Dark*, a collection of essays about social problems. It got a lukewarm reception

Industrialist Andrew Carnegie, who often gave financial aid to public figures he admired, offered Keller an annual pension. She accepted only after she became alarmed about Sullivan's failing health.

from critics and public alike. Keller was criticized for her socialistic views and even for *having* political views. One reviewer said the book was full of errors of judgment, undoubtedly the consequence of the "limitations of [the author's] development."

Meanwhile, more and more editors were rejecting the articles she submitted on the women's movement, on politics, on economics. The world, it seemed, was not interested in what Helen Keller thought about anything but Helen Keller.

Money was becoming a serious problem for Keller and her friends the Macys. To make matters worse, the Macys' seven-year marriage was beginning to show signs of strain. Always a heavy drinker, John Macy was using more alcohol than ever. His wife, slender and pretty when she married, had grown heavy; she was often ill and usually exhausted. The house at Wrentham had become a colder place.

Keller had once again started to take speech lessons. Although she had made

Demonstrating for the right to vote, American women march in New York City in 1912. Keller was a strong supporter of the women's suffrage movement, which gained its objective in 1920.

An intense Keller moves a chessman during a game with Sullivan at Radcliffe. Keller, who learned the game while she was in college, proved to be a formidable competitor.

little progress, she decided to try to earn some money by lecturing. She faced her first audience in Montclair, New Jersey, in 1913. Sullivan was at her side to interpret as she spoke on "The Right Use of Our Senses."

The lecture was a grim ordeal for Keller. "Terror invaded my flesh," she wrote later. "I felt my voice soaring and I knew that meant falsetto; frantically I dragged it down till my words fell about me like loose bricks." She left the stage in tears, sure she had failed miserably. She was wrong: the people in the audience—unheard, of course, by Keller—were applauding wildly. They had taken her to their hearts, and she was launched on a new and successful career that would last for 50 years.

Although her audiences could understand little of what she said, Helen Keller became one of America's best-loved public speakers. She and Sullivan soon developed a format for their appearances. First, "Teacher" would give a brief talk in which she introduced her famous student and described her own methods of educating her. Next, the two would demonstrate how Keller read Sullivan's lips with her fingertips. Finally, Keller would speak directly to the audience, Sullivan repeating her words.

Wherever she spoke, Keller was received by friendly, cheering crowds. After poet Carl Sandburg heard her, he wrote, "It was interesting to watch that audience minute by minute come along till they loved you big and far. . . . Those who hear and see you feel that zest for living, the zest you radiate, is more important than any formula about how to live life."

The First Appearance on the Lecture Platform of

HELEN KELLER

And her Teacher Mrs. Macy (Anne M. Sullivan)

SUBJECT

"The Heart and the Hand," or the Right Use of our Senses

TREMONT TEMPLE, Boston
ONE NIGHT ONLY
MONDAY EVENING, MARCH 24th, at 8:15 P. M.
SEATS, 25c. to $1.50, NOW ON SALE

Keller and Sullivan's 1913 Boston lecture is billed as their "first appearance," but it was actually their second. Their first performance — which terrified Keller — had been in Montclair, New Jersey.

As Keller and Sullivan traveled around the country giving lectures, the Macys' marriage came to an end. John Macy had for some time felt that he had married "an institution" rather than a wife; in 1914 he made it clear that he no longer wished to live with Annie Sullivan. The heartbroken Keller wrote him many letters, begging him to reconsider.

"Have you forgotten all the sunshine, all the laughter, all the long walks, drives, and jolly adventures, all the splendid

After poet Carl Sandburg had attended a Keller-Sullivan lecture in Chicago, he wrote Keller an enthusiastic letter. "I saw and heard you last night at the Palace," he said, "and enjoyed it a thousand ways."

books we read together?" she asked. But Macy's mind was made up, and he never again lived with his wife. The Macys did not get a formal divorce, however, and all three remained friends until John Macy died of a stroke in 1932.

Andrew Carnegie had renewed his offer of an annuity, and Keller had once again declined with a smile. "I haven't been beaten yet," she told him in the spring of 1914. She was, however, increasingly worried about Sullivan's deteriorating health. When her teacher collapsed in a hotel in Maine, where they were giving a lecture, Keller was unable to call for assistance. "My helplessness terrified me," she wrote later. The hotel manager finally appeared, and with his aid the two women boarded a train for Wrentham.

Safely home, Keller wrote a letter to Carnegie, telling him frankly about the episode in Maine and admitting how helpless she had felt. The industrialist sent a check at once, along with a note. "There are a few great souls who can rise to the height of allowing others to do for them what they would like to do for others," he said, adding, "And so you have risen."

Carnegie's gift enabled Keller and Sullivan to hire an assistant. For years, Sullivan alone had maintained their correspondence, balanced the books, taken care of the housekeeping and cooking, answered the endless telephone calls, and dealt with the stream of visitors who turned up at the door of the house in Wrentham. Now, with relief, the ailing teacher and her pupil put a "help-wanted" notice in the newspaper.

One of the first people to respond was a 24-year-old Scotswoman named Polly Thomson. She had just arrived in the United States, had never worked with the handicapped, could not read Braille or the manual alphabet, and had never heard of Helen Keller. She was, however, strong, cheerful, intelligent, and quick to learn. Sullivan and Keller hired her as secretary-housekeeper at once.

Thomson was soon adept at typing, balancing checkbooks, and cooking, and she became an expert at handling dogs, visitors, and timetables. She joined the household in 1914 and managed it with grace and good humor until her death almost 46 years later.

Helen Keller was a staunch pacifist. When war broke out in Europe in 1914, she made it clear that she opposed United States involvement in the conflict. In a 1915 speech in New York City she said, "I look upon the world as my fatherland, and every war has for me the horror of a family feud. I hold true patriotism to be the brotherhood and mutual service of all men."

Keller was by no means the only American to speak out against war, but her views about World War I were unpopular

Keller, who was frequently asked for autographed pictures of herself, inscribed this one to Italian sculptor Onorio Ruotolo in 1908. Ruotolo was one of many sculptors who created likenesses of Keller.

with many of her fellow citizens, particularly after the United States entered the conflict in 1917. Nevertheless, she continued to speak her mind—and she continued to hold her place in Americans' hearts.

"Nothing ever shook the public's conviction," writes one of her biographers, Joseph P. Lash, "that here was someone who wished only to do good, and even more important, someone who had prevailed against the most extraordinary odds, whose joyousness and tenderness had survived some of the greatest trials in American history."

In the fall of 1916, Keller experienced one of the most painful episodes in her life. Her antiwar lectures had been coolly received the previous summer, leaving her in an uncharacteristically discouraged mood. Sullivan was seriously ill; her doctors thought she had tuberculosis and had ordered her to spend the next few months at a New York state health resort. Polly Thomson was to accompany Sullivan, and Kate Keller had just arrived in Wrentham to look after her daughter.

Keller and Sullivan had taken on a temporary secretary to help with their summer lecture trip. He was Peter Fagan, a 29-year-old journalist who shared Keller's views on socialism and pacifism and who had taught himself Braille and the manual language. The 36-year-old Keller found the young man warm and sympathetic, but her mother disliked him. Kate Keller disapproved of her daughter's radical political views, and she considered Fagan's even worse.

One September evening Keller was sitting alone in her study, feeling, as she

Keller sets out on an early-morning jaunt in 1919. Always eager to participate in normal activities, she had taken riding lessons while she was a student at the Wright-Humason School.

than a friendship, will knock at the door of your heart."

Keller had admitted to Bell that she thought of love sometimes, but as "a beautiful flower I must not touch." Bell had refused to accept that answer. "Do not think that because you cannot see or hear, you are debarred from the supreme happiness of women," he had said.

"I cannot imagine a man wanting to marry me," Helen had replied sadly. "I should think it would be like marrying a statue."

This evening, as she sat with Peter Fagan, Keller remembered Bell's words. "If a good man should desire to make you his wife," he had said, "don't let anyone persuade you to forgo that happiness."

Now she was facing just such a desire. Fagan's love, she wrote, "was a bright sun that shone upon my helplessness and isolation. The sweetness of being loved enchanted me, and I yielded to an imperious longing to be part of a man's life." Tremblingly, she signaled her acceptance of Fagan's proposal.

Keller wanted to tell her mother and her teacher "about the wonderful thing that had happened to me," at once, but Fagan thought they should wait. "Certainly they will disapprove at first," he said. "Let us keep our love secret a little while. Your teacher is too ill to be excited just now and we must tell her first."

The happy couple applied for a marriage license, but they said nothing at home for several days. At last Keller could stand the secrecy no more; she told Fagan she was going to give Sullivan the good news before her teacher left for her trip to the health resort. The next morn-

later put it, "utterly despondent," when Fagan entered the room. "For a long time," she wrote, "he held my hand in silence, then he began talking to me tenderly. I was surprised that he cared so much about me.... He was full of plans for my happiness. He said if I would marry him, he would always be near me to help me in the difficulties of life."

Years earlier, Keller's friend Alexander Graham Bell had told her that someday this would happen. "A day must come," he had said, "when love, which is more ing, however, the newspapers broke the story: a reporter had found the marriage-license application at Boston's city hall.

Kate Keller was furious. She stormed into her daughter's room. "What have you been doing with that creature?" she demanded. "The papers are full of a dreadful story about you and him. What does it all mean? Tell me!" Panicked, Helen Keller denied everything. But there was no denying her signature on the document at city hall.

Acting, perhaps, more like the overprotective mother of a teenage girl than the parent of a world-famous, 36-year-old woman, Kate Keller ordered Fagan out of the house. She refused to let the lovers even say good-bye. Then she took her daughter home to Alabama. Learning that the Keller women would travel part of the way by boat, Fagan got word to his fiancée that he would meet her aboard, take her off the boat, and bring her to Florida. There they would be married.

Kate Keller heard about the couple's plan and quickly bought train tickets for herself and her daughter. Fagan made the boat trip by himself. He did not, however, give up. He showed up on the Kellers' front porch in Alabama one morning. Helen Keller greeted him with joy, but her sister's husband leveled his rifle at the young man and forced him to leave.

A week later the family was awakened one night by a noise. Investigating, they found Keller on the porch, a packed bag by her side. She was waiting for Fagan. Her family hustled her inside. Fagan must have realized his case was hopeless; the Kellers never heard from him again.

"It is a terrible picture to me," wrote a sympathetic friend later, "of the blind deaf-mute girl waiting on the porch all night for a lover who never came." Many years later, Keller wrote about the affair. "The brief love will remain in my life," she said, "a little island of joy surrounded by dark waters. I am glad that I have had the experience of being loved and desired."

By the spring of 1917 Annie Sullivan's health was much improved, and she and Keller were reunited. Their finances, however, were in sad shape. The United States had entered the war, and few Americans wanted to hear antiwar sentiments. Revenues from the Keller-Sullivan lectures dropped sharply. The two women decided to economize by selling their Wrentham home and moving to a small house in Queens, New York.

The next year brought promising news. A Hollywood film company asked Keller to star in a movie based on her own life. "Inspirational" films were popular at the moment and Keller, despite her political views, continued to be a heroine to most Americans.

Film executives assured Keller that the movie would give her the opportunity to address a huge audience about the problems of the blind; they also pointed out that she could earn enough money from it to take care of Sullivan if she should outlive her pupil. Keller was immediately receptive to the proposal. "Talkies"— movies with sound—had not yet been invented, and she knew her imperfect speaking voice would be no problem. With her mother and Sullivan, she set out for California.

The trio's stay in Hollywood was exciting. The film community was intrigued

Comedian Charlie Chaplin makes a point on the Hollywood set of Deliverance, *the 1919 movie that starred Helen Keller. Seated are Keller (center), aide Polly Thomson (left), and Annie Sullivan.*

Silent-screen stars Mary Pickford and Douglas Fairbanks greet fans in the 1920s. Like most of the Hollywood community, the two received their unusual new colleague, Helen Keller, with awed enthusiasm.

by Helen Keller, surely one of its most unusual stars. Mary Pickford and Douglas Fairbanks talked to her about making a movie to benefit the blind, and Charlie Chaplin volunteered to act in her picture.

That picture, called *Deliverance*, was a fantastic jumble of sentiment, symbolism, and spectacle. Hoping to appeal to audiences of every taste, the producers included everything from shots of Keller as a baby to Greek mythology to epic battle scenes. *Deliverance* was released in an

avalanche of publicity, but it was a critical and box-office disaster. Sullivan and the Kellers, whose advice about making the film had been ignored, left Hollywood, possibly wiser, certainly poorer.

The Hollywood misadventure had one positive effect. Arthur Keller's suggestion that his daughter and her teacher go on the stage had been indignantly rejected 23 years earlier. Now, in the wake of the publicity surrounding *Deliverance*, the idea of vaudeville began to seem less ab-

This carefully lighted portrait was used to advertise Keller and Sullivan's stage show in the 1920s. Keller enjoyed their theatrical tours, but the ailing Sullivan found them increasingly difficult.

Actress Ethel Barrymore exchanges an introductory handshake with Keller in 1921. Both politically liberal, the two would later work together to help reelect President Franklin D. Roosevelt.

"There is nothing," an observer once noted, "to sadden one in Helen Keller's appearance." Keller liked clothes, and she dressed well, favoring such elegant attire as this fashionable, ostrich-plumed hat.

surd. When a prominent booking agency offered Keller and Sullivan a contract for a highly paid, nationwide theatrical tour in 1919, they accepted.

For the next five years, teacher and pupil traveled around the country, presenting a dignified, 20-minute show in which Sullivan told the story of Keller's education and Keller answered questions from the audience.

While they were appearing in Los Angeles in 1921, Keller received word that her mother had died suddenly in Alabama. "I had not even known she was ill," Keller wrote later. "Every fiber of my being cried out at the thought of facing the audience, but it had to be done." That night she went on stage as scheduled,

giving the audience the same quick, often humorous responses to their questions as usual.

Keller came to enjoy life on the performance circuit, but Sullivan found it increasingly difficult. Her weak eyes were tormented by the glare of the footlights, and more than once she had to cancel a performance because her voice failed. Polly Thomson, who had learned Sullivan's lines, made an acceptable substitute, but Keller felt lost without "Teacher" at her side.

By 1924 Keller's beloved companion was almost as handicapped as she. The time had come, she decided, to turn her efforts to her first mission in life: work for the blind.

At 45, Helen Keller was healthy, energetic, and eager to help the rest of the world. She plunged into a fund-raising campaign for the blind that might have exhausted a nonhandicapped person half her age.

FIVE

Evening

Helen Keller's name was magic. The directors of the American Foundation for the Blind (AFB), a nonprofit organization formed in 1921, were delighted when she agreed to join their staff as a fund-raiser in 1924. At 58, Annie Sullivan was ill, tired, and almost totally blind, but she worked as hard as ever. She and Keller now began to tour the country again, this time seeking out the leaders of American industry, science, and the arts.

The warmth of Keller's personality seemed to melt all hearts. Automobile magnate Henry Ford contributed generously to the Foundation for the Blind, as did multimillionaire oil baron John D. Rockefeller. Leaders of the motion picture industry, who had come to know and admire Keller and Sullivan when they were working in Hollywood, supported their cause with enthusiasm. Cowboy humorist Will Rogers made a series of radio broadcasts in which he asked for contributions for Keller's work. Money rolled in; he sent it to Keller with a note saying, "Don't hesitate to ask for more."

During the three years that Keller and Sullivan worked for the AFB, they spoke to more than a quarter of a million people in 123 cities. Their efforts raised more than $1 million, a spectacular sum in the 1920s. Individual contributions came in all sizes: one Washington millionaire heard Keller speak and promptly wrote out a check for $100,000. Another giver was a crippled teenager, who scraped together $500 for the fund. Hundreds of children broke their piggy banks and sent their pennies to Keller.

Keller's efforts were not limited to the foundation. She had always been distressed by the confusion of reading systems for the blind. Five different systems—European Braille, American Braille, New York Point, Moon Point, and Boston Line Letter—were then in use. She had learned them all, but she saw no reason why other sightless people should have to go to the same trouble. Her eloquent pleas for standardization were largely responsible for the international acceptance in 1932 of Louis Braille's original finger-read alphabet.

Keller's ceaseless travels allowed her to meet people at all economic and political levels. She was invited to the White House by United States presidents from Grover Cleveland to Lyndon Johnson, and all seemed to come under her spell. She brought a smile to the normally poker-faced Calvin Coolidge, and she became a close friend of Franklin and Eleanor Roosevelt. When she met Dwight Eisenhower, she touched his face and said, "You have a beautiful smile." Her gesture brought tears to the president's eyes. "But not much hair," he joked back to cover his emotion, adding quietly, "I am deeply touched at your coming to see me, Miss Keller."

Artists were also touched by Keller and her appreciation of their work. She was particularly responsive to sculpture, which her sensitive hands allowed her to experience directly. "My fingers," she said once, "cannot get the impression of a large whole at a glance, but I feel the parts, and my mind puts them together." Moved by her appreciation, many sculptors portrayed her expressive face.

Keller found genuine pleasure in music, whose rhythms she perceived by placing her fingers on an instrument as it was played, on the lips of a singer, or on a radio speaker. When opera star Enrico Caruso sang for her, they both cried. "I have sung the best in my life for you, Helen Keller!" exclaimed the famed tenor.

Jascha Heifetz gave a private concert for Keller, allowing her to rest her fingers on his violin. "Each delicate note alighted on my fingertips like thistledown," she wrote later. "They touched my face, my hair, like kisses remembered."

Keller's sensitive fingertips interpret a book printed in Braille. Thanks largely to her efforts, Braille was accepted in 1932 as the world's standard alphabet for the blind.

Keller listens with her fingers as tenor Lauritz Melchior, costumed for his role in Tristan and Isolde, *sings an aria at the Metropolitan Opera in New York City in 1941.*

Many artists, scientists, and intellec- tuals were drawn to Annie Sullivan as well as to her pupil. The great physicist Albert Einstein said, "Your work, Mrs. Macy, has interested me more than any other achievement in modern education. You not only imparted language to Helen Keller but you unfolded her personality, and such work has in it an element of the superhuman."

Dr. Maria Montessori, the Italian edu- cator who revolutionized modern teach- ing methods, agreed with Einstein. At a ceremony in which both she and Sullivan were being honored for their educational breakthroughs, she pointed to Keller's teacher and said, "I have been called a pioneer, but there is your pioneer."

Not all Keller and Sullivan's encounters were so friendly. They were both great admirers of George Bernard Shaw's plays, particularly *Pygmalion* (the source of *My Fair Lady*) and *St. Joan*. When the two women visited London, in 1932, they called on socialite Lady Nancy Astor, who introduced them to her friend Shaw.

The American women were thrilled. "I'm so happy to meet you," said Keller to the British playwright. "I've wanted to know you for ever so long." Shaw replied, "Why do all you Americans say the same thing?"

Ignoring the taunt, Keller urged the au- thor to visit America. "Why should I?" he asked. "All America comes to see me." Astor shook his arm. "Shaw," she said, "don't you realize that this is Helen Keller? She is deaf and blind."

"Why, of course!" snapped Shaw. "All Americans are deaf and blind—and dumb." Shocked, Sullivan slowly spelled the playwright's words into Keller's hand.

Newspaper reports of the meeting stirred international criticism of Shaw. The sharp-tongued writer insisted—no doubt sincerely—that he had been mis- interpreted. He had only wanted, he said, to "avoid any air of sympathizing with Miss Keller as an unfortunate person," and to make her feel "that she was a highly distinguished visitor." Neverthe- less, his words had stung. "He was not," observed his visitor sadly, "particularly gracious to me."

Such disappointments, however, never bothered Keller for long. She continued to devote her vast energy to her work and—more and more as they grew older—to her beloved teacher.

Sullivan was beginning to need almost as much care as Keller had required when the two first met. Impatient with Braille, which she had never learned to read easily, Sullivan spent much time tell- ing Keller about her own unhappy child- hood. Keller had not known of her teacher's early trials, and she was ap- palled. She was also terrified by Sullivan's declining health: how could she live with- out her?

Although Sullivan had, as she put it, "no religion at all," her pupil was deeply religious. At the age of 16, she had been introduced to the doctrines of Emmanuel Swedenborg, a Swedish mystic who taught that the essence of God is love, wisdom, and strength.

Swedenborgianism included the belief that death was followed by rebirth—into a life where the lame would walk, the

(text continues on page 89)

Not yet aware that British playwright George Bernard Shaw has spoken cruelly to her, Helen Keller smiles serenely. Shaw's friend, Lady Nancy Astor (right), was shocked by his remarks.

Amused by his guest's words, President Calvin Coolidge cracks a rare smile in 1926. Helen Keller had just said, "They say you are cold, but you are not. You are a dear president."

Keller, who had first visited the White House when she was seven years old, joins President Herbert Hoover after a meeting of the World Conference for the Blind in 1931.

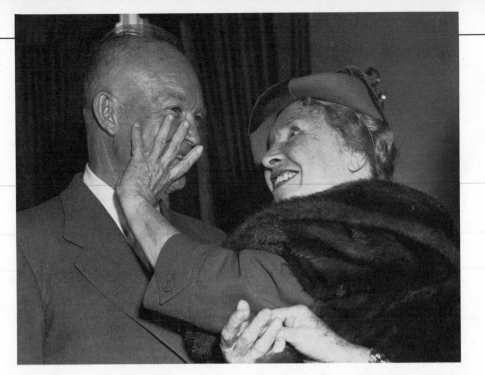

President Dwight Eisenhower responds with a grin after Keller asks to "see your celebrated smile." Keller's right hand is extended to Polly Thomson, who translates the president's words for her friend.

Keller inspires another presidential smile as she chats with John F. Kennedy at the White House in 1961. Looking on is AFB official Evelyn Seide.

Visiting the studio of her friend Jo Davidson (right) in 1950, Keller examines his unfinished sculpture of President Franklin D. Roosevelt. Davidson also made several portraits of Keller.

blind see. It was a faith perfectly suited to Keller's way of thinking, and she became a fervent, lifelong believer.

"The spiritual world offers no difficulty," she wrote, "to one who is deaf and blind. Nearly everything in the natural world is as vague, as remote from my senses, as spiritual things seem to the minds of most people."

By the summer of 1925, Sullivan's eyesight was reduced to 10 percent of normal, and she was easily tired. As Sullivan's body grew weaker, Keller's faith grew stronger. In 1927, she explained her beliefs in *My Religion*, a book that has been often reprinted and widely read by people of many faiths ever since. "I cannot imagine myself without religion," she wrote. "I could as easily fancy a living body without a heart."

Sullivan had never enjoyed fund-raising. As her companion's health faded, Keller too began to find their work for the American Foundation for the Blind burdensome. In a letter to her sister at the end of 1924 she said, "Oh my, what a strenuous business this beggar's life is!" Nevertheless, she continued to travel, lecture, and write for the AFB until the end of 1927, when Sullivan was no longer able to keep up the strenuous pace.

Aided by Sullivan, Keller spent much of the next two years writing *Midstream*, the second volume of her autobiography. It was a struggle, but she retained her sense of humor. In a letter to a friend, she said, "*Midstream* is giving me more trouble than a Chinese funeral, what with a new host of letters, a torrent of books to be autographed, and interviews to be given. Getting out a book is worse than any kind of funeral when I come to think of it—at least we don't know how much trouble we are to others when we are dead."

Midstream, which appeared in 1929, was an immediate success with literary critics and the public. After publication, Keller, Sullivan, and Polly Thomson made the first of several trips to Europe. Keller was excited by the new experience, but her companions were somewhat less enthusiastic. "Polly and I decided," said Sullivan in a letter home, "that Helen's insides must be made of cast iron fastened down with hoops of steel; she wasn't a bit affected by the food or drink or heat."

Sullivan's deteriorating eyesight required that she undergo yet another operation; her surgery was performed in April 1936. Sullivan's sight was not improved this time, and the procedure further weakened the frail, 70-year-old woman. By the fall of that year, it was clear that she was dying.

At Sullivan's bedside on October 15, 1936, Polly Thomson wrote down what were to be "Teacher's" last words. "I wanted to be loved," she said. "I was lonesome—then Helen came into my life. I wanted her to love me and I loved her. Then later Polly came and I loved Polly and we were always so happy together.... Thank God I gave up my life that Helen might live. God help her to live without me when I go."

Annie Sullivan died on October 20. Keller, of course, had known she would soon lose her lifetime companion, but the

Polly Thomson gives Keller a dancing lesson in 1921. Efficient and good natured, Thomson was Keller's secretary, bodyguard, housekeeper, lecture assistant, and friend for 45 years.

Helen's hands—saw and with a quickened heartbeat knew what I had seen—Helen—think of it—Helen comforting her companion."

Many of Keller's friends and associates thought Sullivan's death would mean the end of Keller's public life. They assumed that she now had no alternative but to go home and live with her sister in Alabama. They were mistaken.

The grief-stricken Keller knew she still had important work to do. She remained on the staff of the AFB as adviser and fund-raiser, and with Thomson at her side, she continued to write and travel. When the director of the Lighthouse for the Blind in Osaka, Japan, begged her to come and work with the blind in his country, she said yes. In 1937 she and Thomson left for the Orient, beginning what would be the first of many world tours.

Keller was famous in Japan. When she arrived in Yokohama, she was met by top government officials and a crowd that included several thousand schoolchildren, all waving Japanese and American flags. "No foreign visitor," reported the *Akita Journal*, "had ever been accorded such an enthusiastic reception."

knowledge made it no easier. She was emotionally shattered. "The light, the music, and the glory of life had been withdrawn," she wrote later.

Journalist Alexander Woolcott was among the mourners at Sullivan's funeral. He wrote of seeing Keller and Thomson follow the casket, "tears pouring down Miss Thomson's cheeks." Then, he said, "I saw the swift, bird-like flittering of

Keller gave 97 lectures in 39 Japanese cities, speaking both of her hopes for world peace and of the needs of the handicapped. She was honored wherever she went. The emperor and empress, who rarely received foreign visitors, invited her to the imperial palace, and in the ancient city of Nara she was allowed to run her hand over the great bronze Buddha. She was the first woman permitted to touch the sacred statue.

Former British Prime Minister Winston Churchill and his wife, Clementine, congratulate Keller in 1955, when she turned 75. Her birthday produced a flood of good wishes from people around the world.

Staff members show Keller a work table at Brooklyn's Industrial Home for the Blind. Insisting that the blind could be self-supporting, Keller campaigned hard for funds to train sightless workers.

When she returned to the United States, Keller settled down to finish writing *Journal*, the new autobiographical account she had been composing for several years. Published in 1938, it was received with the same high praise as her earlier volumes. One critic wrote, "This book answers effectually the question,'What will Helen Keller do without Teacher?' "

Soon after the publication of *Journal*,

Keller and Thomson moved to Westport, Connecticut. Their new house, a gift from the American Foundation for the Blind, enchanted Keller. "We have never loved a place more," she wrote a friend. "I am especially delighted with my study, which has spacious bookshelves, 35 cubbyholes, and windows hospitable to the sun."

Keller had long planned to write a biography of Annie Sullivan. Established in

Visiting Japan with Polly Thomson (back to camera) in 1948, Keller examines a statue of a dog in Tokyo. The Japanese people's love for animals, she said, testified to their love for humanity.

"Listening" to radio music with one hand, Keller keeps time with the other. Although she could not recognize individual melodies, she was able to receive the rhythmic pulse of music through vibrations.

her new home, she assembled letters, diaries, and notes, and began the book. She spent every free moment writing it, but as it turned out, her tribute to Sullivan would not be finished for almost 20 years. (Keller's manuscript, almost completed, was destroyed in a fire in 1946. Unhappy but undefeated, she started the book all over again. *Teacher: Anne Sullivan Macy* was finally published in 1955.)

Keller had passionately opposed war all her life, but on December 7, 1941, when the Japanese bombed Pearl Harbor, the U.S. naval base on the Hawaiian island of Oahu, she was as outraged as the rest of America. She wanted desperately to be part of her nation's World War II struggle.

At first, it seemed unlikely that a middle-aged blind and deaf woman could contribute much to the war effort, but by

Egypt's education minister, who was also blind, welcomes Keller to Cairo in 1952. "Our merciful God," said another blind Egyptian leader, "gave us Louis Braille for one eye, and Helen Keller for the other."

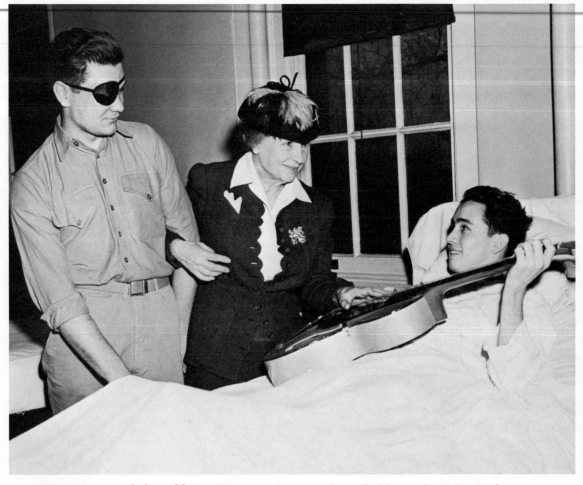

Keller visits wounded World War II veterans in 1946. She called her military hospital tours — which were obviously much appreciated by the soldiers — "the crowning experience of my life."

1943 Keller had found a role uniquely suited to her abilities. She began to tour military hospitals, giving advice and encouragement to men who had been blinded or deafened in the war.

By now Keller was almost a legend; most of the men she visited had known of her since they were children, and they were impressed by meeting her in per-

son. As Eleanor Roosevelt observed, "Just to know of her presence seemed to encourage the boys." Keller's visits to the wounded, added the president's wife, were "probably the most healing that can come to them."

The visits were "healing" to Keller as well. She was deeply touched when she realized how much good she could do

On the eve of her departure for a Far Eastern tour in 1955, Keller reads the lips of her friend Eleanor Roosevelt. The former first lady called her "America's goodwill ambassador to the world."

with "a kiss or a laying of my hand on a weary head." She later described her long and exhausting hospital tours as "the crowning experience of my life."

Keller kept up her hospital visits after the war ended in 1945. She also continued to work with the AFB and its offshoot, the American Foundation for the Overseas Blind (now called Helen Keller International). Between 1946 and 1957, she and Polly Thomson visited hospitals and schools in 35 countries on five continents, helping to organize and promote programs for the handicapped.

In the United States, she remained as active as ever. Perhaps most important to her was the work she did for those who shared her own affliction. At her urging, the AFB created a new training program for the deaf-blind, whom Keller called "the loneliest human beings on earth."

Once considered uneducatable, these doubly handicapped people were often sent to mental institutions. Today, largely due to Helen Keller's efforts, many schools in the United States offer special training for deaf-blind children. They have come to be recognized as individuals who can be taught many of the same skills as ordinary youngsters.

Helen Keller's reputation continued to expand. As she grew older, nations around the world flooded her with appreciation. She received France's Legion of Honor, Brazil's Southern Cross, the Philippines' Golden Heart, and Japan's Sacred Treasure award.

In the United States, Keller was show-

Keller squeezes oranges in her Westport home in 1955. Usually up at five in the morning, she began her days by bringing flowers from the garden, making her bed, taking a walk, and helping to make breakfast.

ered with medals from civic organizations. In 1964 President Lyndon Johnson gave her the nation's highest civilian award, the Presidential Medal of Freedom. Keller received honorary degrees from Harvard as well as from universities in Scotland, Germany, India, and South Africa.

In 1957 Polly Thomson suffered a cerebral hemorrhage from which she never truly recovered. She died in 1960. Once again, Keller had lost a loyal and almost indispensable friend. She was now 80 years old, and more philosophical than she had been at the time of Annie Sullivan's death.

In a letter to Thomson's brother, Keller said, "Now I sit by her empty chair thinking of the fidelity with which she helped me in my difficult work and the tireless

Realizing she has Polly Thomson (right) stumped, Keller flashes a triumphant smile during a 1956 checkers match. The game, which they played on a specially designed board, was a favorite pastime of the two women.

Mildred Tyson, Helen Keller's younger sister, meets Patty Duke, the actress who played Helen in the 1960 Broadway play The Miracle Worker. *Duke holds the doll that represented Tyson in the drama.*

Helen Keller's Westport, Connecticut, house looks much as it did when she occupied it. Her original Westport home, built in 1938, was destroyed by fire in 1946; the building shown here is its successor.

cheer with which she took part in our amazing adventures. I am sure that now that they have met in heaven, Teacher is prouder of Polly than ever."

Helen Keller's many years of activity were coming to an end. In 1961 she accepted the Humanitarian of the Year award from the Lions Club International; it was her last important public appearance. Later that year, she suffered a mild stroke. From that point on, she stayed at home in Connecticut.

Still mentally active, Keller continued to read her favorite books—the Bible and works of poetry and philosophy—and to write. Friends visited and kept her informed about world events, and AFB representatives brought her regular reports of the foundation's progress.

Keller had always kept at least one dog,

(text continues on page 105)

"Feeling" the beauty of the dance, a delighted Helen Keller stands amid a troupe of dancers in 1954. With her (in long gown) is choreographer Martha Graham.

Keller takes part in a spirited conversation a few years before her death in 1968. She remained curious, enthusiastic, and energetic until almost the end of her life.

and in her last years she continued to walk in the fields with her pets. A guide rail enabled her to take long walks around the grounds in safety. She strolled in her garden every morning, stroking the flowers as she and Sullivan had done in Tuscumbia 80 years earlier.

A secretary-companion replaced Polly Thomson. Keller had always known she needed help and had always accepted it gratefully, but at 87, as at 17, she remained as independent as her handicaps allowed. Suffering a series of minor strokes in the early 1960s, she began to grow frail. "My poor darling is walking that last mile so very slowly," wrote her companion to a friend in late 1967.

Keller died quietly on June 1, 1968, a few weeks before her 88th birthday. Her ashes were placed alongside those of Annie Sullivan and Polly Thomson in Washington, D.C.'s National Cathedral.

Through her writing and her public appearances, Helen Keller profoundly altered the world's treatment and education of the handicapped. But it was simply as a personal presence that she made her greatest impact. Her life of dedicated service and her demonstration of the power of the human spirit over the most crushing adversity have inspired the world for almost a century.

Helen Keller's life might have been one of silent obscurity. If Annie Sullivan had not thrown open the door, and if Keller had not stepped boldly and joyously through it, she might have remained the wordless "no-child" in a "no-land"—as she described herself—that Sullivan first encountered.

With a rare combination of courage, intelligence, and sensitivity, Keller faced the terrors of the unknown and unknowable world and mastered them. She learned to swim, to ride a bicycle and a horse. She flew in an open-cockpit airplane and went on camping trips. She was never known to shrink from danger. "Life," she once wrote, "is either a daring adventure or nothing."

FURTHER READING

Brooks, Van Wyck. *Helen Keller: Sketch for a Portrait*. New York: E. P. Dutton, 1956.

Harrity, Richard, and Ralph G. Martin. *The Three Lives of Helen Keller*. New York: Doubleday, 1962.

Keller, Helen. *Journal*. New York: Doubleday, Doran, 1938.

———. *Midstream: My Later Life*. New York: Doubleday, Doran, 1929.

———. *My Religion*. New York: Doubleday, Doran, 1927.

———. *Out of the Dark*. New York: Doubleday, Page, 1913.

———. *The Story of My Life*. New York: Doubleday, Page, 1903.

———. *Teacher: Anne Sullivan Macy*. New York: Doubleday, 1955.

———. *The World I Live In*. New York: Century, 1908.

Lash, Joseph P. *Helen and Teacher: The Story of Helen Keller and Anne Sullivan Macy*. New York: Delacorte, 1980.

Ross, Ishbel. *Journey Into Light*. New York: Appleton-Century-Crofts, 1951.

White, Helen Elmira. *Valiant Companions: Helen Keller and Anne Sullivan Macy*. Philadelphia: Macrae Smith, 1959.

CHRONOLOGY

June 27, 1880	Helen Adams Keller born in Tuscumbia, Alabama
February 1882	Loses sight and hearing after illness
March 1887	Annie Sullivan hired to teach Helen
July 1887	Keller begins to learn Braille
1888	Visits Perkins Institution in Boston with Sullivan
1894	Begins study at Wright-Humason School in New York City
1896	Arthur Keller, father, dies
	Keller enters the Cambridge School for Young Ladies
1900	Enrolls at Radcliffe College
1903	Publishes *The Story of My Life*
1904	Graduates from Radcliffe
1905	Sullivan marries John Macy
1908	Keller publishes *The World I Live In*
1913	Publishes *Out of the Dark*
	Embarks on lecture tour with Sullivan
1914	Sullivan and John Macy separate; Polly Thomson hired
1918–19	Keller stars in the film *Deliverance*
1919–24	Appears on vaudeville circuit with Sullivan
1921	Kate Adams Keller, mother, dies
1924	Keller begins work for the American Foundation for the Blind
1927	Publishes *My Religion*
1929	Publishes *Midstream*
1936	Sullivan dies
1937	Keller tours Japan with Thomson
1938	Publishes *Journal*
1943–46	Tours military hospitals
1946–57	Visits 35 countries on behalf of handicapped
1955	Publishes *Teacher: Anne Sullivan Macy*
1960	Thomson dies
1961	Keller suffers a stroke; retires from public life
June 1, 1968	Dies in Westport, Connecticut

INDEX

PICTURE CREDITS

Dennis Wepman has a graduate degree in linguistics from Columbia University and has written widely on sociology, linguistics, popular culture, and American folklore. He now teaches English at Queens College of the City University of New York. He is the author of several volumes in the Chelsea House series WORLD LEADERS PAST & PRESENT.

❖　❖　❖

Matina S. Horner is president of Radcliffe College and associate professor of psychology and social relations at Harvard University. She is best known for her studies of women's motivation, achievement, and personality development. Dr. Horner serves on several national boards and advisory councils, including those of the National Science Foundation, Time Inc., and the Women's Research and Education Institute. She earned her B. A. from Bryn Mawr College and Ph.D. from the University of Michigan, and holds honorary degrees from many colleges and universities, including Mount Holyoke, Smith, Tufts, and the University of Pennsylvania.

DATE DUE